About the Author

Paul Devereux is an international expert on Earth Mysteries. He has researched and written over a dozen books on the subject and has lectured all over the world. His other titles include *Earth Lights*, *Earthmind*, *Shamanism and the Mystery Lines*, *Places of Power*, *Earth Memory*, *Secrets of the Ancient and Sacred Places* and *Symbolic Landscapes*.

Earth Mysteries

Piatkus Guides

A PIATKUS GUIDE

Earth Mysteries

Paul Devereux

PIATKUS

© 1999 Paul Devereux

First published in 1999 by
Judy Piatkus (Publishers) Ltd
5 Windmill Street, London W1P 1HF
E-mail: info@piatkus.co.uk

**For the latest news and information on all our titles
visit our new website at www.piatkus.co.uk**

The moral rights of the author have been asserted

A catalogue record for this book is available from the British Library

ISBN 0-7499-2035-1

Typeset by Action Publishing Technology Limited, Gloucester
Printed and bound in Great Britain by
Mackays of Chatham PLC

Contents

Introduction

'Earth Mysteries' is a general term for the broad subject area relating to the wonders and enigmas of the distant past. It can range from simple fascination with old sacred places and speculation about archaeological puzzles, to the rediscovery and personal application of principles contained in the nearly lost knowledge of ancient societies. In short, Earth Mysteries is a modern attempt to uncover the wisdom of the ancient mind and apply some of the truths it contained. The term itself was coined in 1974, when it appeared as a headline in *The Whole Earth Catalog* (an American underground publication started in the 1960s which published articles on the alternative scene) alongside a grainy black and white photograph of Stonehenge.

Earth Mysteries is not some specific traditional technique you can learn to 'do', but is an area of enquiry that encompasses many approaches to the understanding of antiquity; it is *multi-disciplinary*. In addition, it involves different ways of working, from intellectual learning and analytical thought at one extreme, to the use of direct experience, intuition, and primary sensing at the other. So, not only is Earth Mysteries a multi-disciplinary subject area, it is also *multi-mode*.

The Purpose of this Guide

Because of its inclusive nature, people's perceptions of what comprises Earth Mysteries vary considerably, rather like the blind men's attempt to describe an elephant to one another by touching different parts of the creature. One view of the Earth Mysteries elephant is that it is a form of neopaganism. When we are looking at prehistoric monuments we are naturally going back to a time before there were any major, global religions, so by definition they are pagan, but Earth Mysteries is not a religious persuasion, pagan or otherwise. Then there are people who are interested in crop circles, ley lines, dowsing, and so forth. They are usually only familiar with the New Age literature, and so get a very distorted view of Earth Mysteries; they think it is all about 'energies', 'touchy-feely' New Age spirituality, notions about being stewards of the Earth, and similar sentiments. There *are* natural Earth energies to consider within the scope of Earth Mysteries, as we will discover, and there are numerous psychological and environmental aspects to the subject area, but the New Age approach by itself is unbalanced, and is frequently based on hoary old myths rather than solid information.

At the other extreme are the analytical types who like to measure and record, monitor and survey. This sort of person often sees ancient monuments as being early astronomical observatories, the birthplaces of modern science. In fact, such sites were more to do with ritual and cosmological functions than anything we might recognise as science today. While a measure of intellectual discipline is essential, the analysts nevertheless overstate their approach. Similarly, the orthodox archaeological view is limited to very restricted notions about ancient people and their skills. Fortunately, a new wind is blowing through archaeology today, and the younger generation are much more prepared to think creatively about the material remains of the past they confront and try to interpret. This trend is generally labelled 'cognitive archaeology', and represents a genuine attempt to get inside the ancient mind. However, despite this change for the better in academic circles, there is still mainstream resistance to anyone going too far down this path, and as the Earth Mysteries area is usually thought to be too far, it tends to be ridiculed or dismissed altogether by many academics. Nevertheless, the more adventurous cognitive archaeologists and the more disciplined Earth Mysteries researchers have much in common.

Given all these confusions and conflicting interests, the most important purpose of this book is simply to explain the background to Earth Mysteries, to identify the main themes, and help you to discern what is authentic from some of the prejudices and modern myths that have grown up within and around the subject area. It will also provide examples of how some of the basic principles contained in ancient wisdom can be adapted for your own personal development today.

Overall, then, this guide tries to reflect the range of content and approach embraced by Earth Mysteries, sometimes offering objective items of information, while at other times presenting more subjective, intuitive and experiential material. One side of the equation without the other leaves the understanding of Earth Mysteries unbalanced and incomplete.

About the Author

My involvement in Earth Mysteries goes back a long way, and was precipitated by a spectacular event that will stay with me all my days. In the mid-1960s I was an art student in Kent, just south of 'Swinging London'. It was a wild, psyche-delic time. It was also a period that coincided with a huge, global 'wave' of UFO sightings; all kinds of people were seeing strange objects in the sky, not just the stereotypical hippy in tie-dyed clothing.

On the evening of 16 May 1967, I was working late in the top-floor studio of Ravensbourne College of Art. There was a scattering of other students, none of whom had ingested anything stronger than coffee from the college canteen. Not wanting to turn on the studio lights, I was working by a north-facing window when a bright orange light in the sky suddenly caught my attention. The light approached steadily. It glowed with the colours of embers, and was a perfectly regular, upright rectangle in shape, having similar propor-tions to a standard door. I had a deep sense of panic when the glowing lightform came to a halt over the fields near the college. As I looked up at the object, I croaked out to the other students to come and see. There were gasps of aston-ishment. By now, other students were coming out onto the car park four floors below, gazing skywards. The glowing orange rectangle seemed to dim slightly, and then its clear outlines softened. It started a kind of churning action, trans-forming through many shapes. The phenomenon finally collapsed into a small, softly glowing cloud that dulled to a rosy glow and gradually dissolved.

It was suggested that what we had witnessed was a flying saucer. It had not occurred to me until then that this event had anything to do with such a thing. To me, a flying saucer was an alien machine, but this had been a *phenomenon* of some inexplicable kind, and seemed more visionary than mechani-cal in nature. Indeed, had I seen the thing on my own, I would have assumed it to be a hallucination and kept quiet.

It became important to me to try to understand what had happened. I scoured many books on UFOs, but felt what was being discussed in them was nothing to do with what I had seen. Then I came across *The Flying Saucer Vision* by John Michell, which had been published that same year, 1967. I liked the word 'vision'. The book mentioned leys and Stonehenge and other Earth Mysteries topics, and I became hooked. A couple of years later, Michell published his seminal work, *The View Over Atlantis*, and journalist Paul Screeton took on the editorship of *The Ley Hunter* journal, the pioneering Earth Mysteries specialist journal to which I subscribed. I began visiting prehistoric sites in earnest and did paintings of them. Eventually, I began writing pieces for *The Ley Hunter*, and in 1976, at Screeton's request, I took on the editorship. I was thrown into the 'front line', and began a steep learning curve. I was to stay as editor for 20 years, and over that time had to distinguish belief, wish-fulfilment and fantasy from what really needed explaining and experiencing. As the years passed, there were arguments and clashes of various kinds (I soon found that people did not like their beliefs disturbed, let alone challenged), we organised annual conferences called 'Ley Hunter Moots', and I wrote many books on Earth Mysteries and related topics. I also became founder/director of the Dragon Project (see Chapter 4) in order to study first-hand the rumours of strange energies at ancient sites.

Over the decades, this full-time involvement has caused me to read a great deal of relevant literature, conduct field-work and scholarly studies, and meet with researchers and knowledge-holders of many persuasions and backgrounds, from academics to indigenous people. I have explored ancient sacred places in many corners of the world, and have approached the mystery of ancient sites from just about every angle – clutching dowsing rods at one extreme, and Geiger counters at the other. I have also had some intense personal experiences at ancient sacred sites, places that have become my teachers in so many ways.

The following pages are offered as a distillation of this research and life experience, and I hope it will be of use to you. It may be that some cherished beliefs or ideas you hold about Earth Mysteries are challenged, but you are of course free to take or leave the information provided here. I can promise that all you will read in this book is honest and authentic. Life is short, and it seems to me that the only mysteries worth tackling are real ones.

1

The Roots of Earth Mysteries

The fascination generated by prehistoric sites as well as the mysterious ancient world that gave rise to them began much earlier than today's interest in Earth Mysteries. First, there was folklore: countryfolk have always viewed prehistoric monuments with wonder and a little fear, and told fireside stories about them. Out of folklore arose the phenomenon of antiquarianism, what the 16th-century scholar, William Camden, called 'the backward-looking curiosity'.

Druidism and Astrology: The Antiquarian Romance

In Britain, antiquarianism emerged during the reign of Elizabeth I, and grew rapidly. A rising sense of patriotism led to the development of a legendary history of Britain, and interest in the visible antiquities of the British countryside acquired a high profile among the educated classes. Two influential works, Camden's *Britannia* of 1586, and

Drayton's *Poly Olbion, Great Britaine* of 1613, established notions about the Druids – Iron Age pagan Celtic priests, seers and magistrates – which were to colour antiquarian interpretation of megalithic monuments. In 1648, the scholar and writer John Aubrey was the first to openly associate stone circles with the Druids, and, more usefully, he was the first to notice that the large stones – megaliths – in and around the village of Avebury in Wiltshire were the remnants of a vast monumental complex. Up until then they had been seen simply as random features and handy sources of building materials. Almost a century later, William Stukeley, probably the most influential antiquarian of his day, asserted that the stones of Avebury formed the image of a great serpent in the landscape. Despite such notions, we owe a debt to Stukeley for his drawings and plans of the Avebury complex and other monuments that have since disappeared; he was outraged when he saw old standing stones being deliberately destroyed by farmers. Stukeley was also the first to record the curious prehistoric earthen avenues he called 'cursuses' (see Chapter 8), and to note correctly the summer solstice sunrise orientation of Stonehenge.

Stukeley served as Secretary to the Society of Antiquaries, which had a close relationship with Freemasonry. John Wood, the architect of Bath, was Stukeley's contemporary and antiquarian rival. He became enamoured of ancient monuments, especially Stonehenge and the megalithic complex of Stanton Drew in Somerset. Wood incorporated elements of numerology and measurement that he discerned in these monuments into his designs for the King's Circus and Royal Crescent in Bath. In addition, the parapet all around the Circus is punctuated by giant stone acorns – a coy reference to the association of Druids with oak groves. It is also thought that in Wood's mind the Crescent represented the moon, and the Circus the sun, for he believed that natural hills and the old monuments had been invested with planetary symbolism in ancient times and he wanted to perpetuate these ideas. Such associations continued to develop. In 1770, a Dr John Smith wrote a book which claimed that Stonehenge had been a 'Temple for Observing the Motions of the Heavenly Bodies'. Other writers and researchers of the period made similar statements about prehistoric sites; one idea was that Stonehenge was part of a vast planetary design marked out by various monuments across Salisbury Plain.

The antiquarian Druid romance reached a further level of manifestation in the late 18th century with the Welshman, Edward Williams, who styled himself as Iolo Morganwg. Although a learned man, he invented an imaginary past unrelated to the actual Druids and their rituals. Around 1780, he implied that he had rediscovered the plans of the traditional Gorsedd circle, the place of bardic assembly, which he said was a circular arrangement of 19 stones with a central pillar and outliers to the east. Williams asserted that Druidism had survived in his locality, Glamorgan, from prehistoric times, and that he and another fellow, Edward Evans, were the only two ordained bards of the old tradition. In 1792, he organised a Gorsedd on Primrose Hill, London, where he made a small-scale stone circle from pebbles. He took these with him when he attended the Eisteddfod (the Welsh national festival of music and poetry) in Carmarthen in 1819, and again held a Gorsedd there, attended by robed and beribboned bardic initiates. It created quite an impression, and not too many years passed until the Gorsedd circle became attached to the Eisteddfod as a matter of course. Today, you can travel around Wales and see the modern stone circles left over from past Eisteddfods.

The modern white-robed 'Druids' who famously attend the summer solstice at Stonehenge are ultimately derived from Williams's Welsh fantasy, or parallels of it. They do not embody a genuine continuity of prehistoric traditions, and their rituals and ideas are modern inventions or beliefs. With that understood, it is nevertheless ironic that scholars now admit the possibility that Iron Age (first millennium BC) Celtic Druidic traditions might have contained elements that originated thousands of years earlier, even reaching back to the Neolithic megalithic builders themselves.

Antiquarianism in Other Lands

While many British antiquarians were attempting to understand or, more often, imagine the pagan religion of their native land and interpret its ancient monuments, there was also antiquarian interest elsewhere. Scandinavian and Dutch antiquarians dug around prehistoric megalithic monuments looking for the bones of giants, and there was much speculation about runic monuments. By the 18th century, the Swedes and others had set up antiquarian societies. As in England, collections of ancient objects were assembled in various European countries, initiating the concept of the museum. From the end of the 18th century the Danes evolved the idea of classifying prehistoric remains by the 'Three Age System' – Stone, Bronze, and Iron – a method still used today for a broad classification of prehistory, itself a term (*prehistoire*) coined by the French in 1833.

In the 18th century, it was fashionable for budding scholars and artists to make the Grand Tour of the classical sites of the Mediterranean region – the ruins of Rome, the temples of Greece. Some Europeans even reached further afield, to the mighty stone ruins of Baalbek in Lebanon, and the remains of Persepolis in Iran, but it was Egypt, littered with the evocative ruins of a great ancient civilisation, that attracted most antiquarian interest. The Great Pyramid, in particular, became the focus of much speculation, its remarkably accurate construction and orientation to the compass points provoking ideas of an advanced but lost civilisation, similar to Atlantis. Antiquarians have perceived units of ancient measurements, ratios, and geometry in the monument's structure, they have argued that it sits in the centre of the world's landmass, that it can be decoded to provide prophecies and lost histories, and, of course, that it has astronomical orientations built into it. There is probably some truth in certain of these ideas, and none in others.

America, too, was not without its antiquarian romance. The early settlers encountered great mounds and earthworks we now know were left by people such as the Hopewell Indians almost 2,000 years ago. However, American antiquarians of the 18th century argued among themselves as to whether the earthworks had indeed been built by indigenous Native American peoples, or a 'lost race', such as one of the lost tribes of Israel, or survivors from Atlantis. This allowed some white Americans to consider the Native Americans as savages, incapable of being descendants of people who could have built the mighty earthen monuments.

Even the third president of the United States, Thomas Jefferson, was unsure who had built the mounds, and in 1784 he ordered the excavation of an Indian mound, employing a sophisticated approach to the digging by cutting trenches and observing what was in the layers revealed in their walls. This method anticipated modern archaeological techniques of stratified excavation. He also urged excavators to make careful plans, drawings and notes so as to record accurately anything that was found. Further, he was aware that the annular rings making up a tree trunk could be used for dating purposes where a tree was found growing out of a site; this foreshadowed tree-ring dating ('dendrochronology') that was to become a major technique in modern archaeology. Despite all this, Jefferson remained unsure as to the origins of America's earthen monuments.

Into the Twentieth Century

There was a parting of the ways within the Western intellect at the end of the 19th century. Religious fundamentalism had gradually and painfully been supplanted by rationalism and science, but this led to many people experiencing a spiritual vacuum, which in turn caused them to seek deeper truths in various forms of occultism. The influential occult movement known as Theosophy was created on the back of the emergence of spiritualism, and it prospered during the early decades of the 20th century, attracting numerous intellectuals. It introduced oriental religious themes such as reincarnation, the law of karma, meditation, and suchlike to a broader audience in the West, and also encouraged an increased interest in the paranormal. But the founders of the Theosophical movement gave much of this material their own spin, based on their personal beliefs, and there was a scandal when it was revealed that one of the movement's leaders, Madam Blavatsky, had faked supposed paranormal feats. She subscribed to the notion that there had been several 'root-races' (an occult belief in the original races of Earth, who existed before accepted history), and she taught that some of these had variously emerged from Atlantis and other mythical lost continents such as Mu in the Pacific, and Lemuria in the Indian Ocean.

The effect of Theosophical influence was to encourage

those with antiquarian leanings to add occult notions and a heightened belief in Atlantis to their ideas about Druids. The idea of Atlantis had first arisen in the works of the ancient Greek philosopher, Plato. It was a supposed continent in the Atlantic with an advanced civilisation which was wiped out in a natural cataclysm. It became a theme for European intellectuals and poets throughout the 17th and 18th centuries, and was popularised in the 19th century by Ignatius Donnelly, a US congressman, in *Atlantis: The Antediluvian World* (1882). He felt that the cultures in the Old and New Worlds had derived from the common source of Atlantis, citing the pyramids in central America and Egypt, and common legends of a flood among his evidence. Many authors followed in his footsteps, notable among them the British author Lewis Spence.

Some of the 'new antiquarians' of the early 20th century would visit ancient sites along with clairvoyants, who claimed to be able to look back in time and see what went on at such places. A common claim among these psychics was that their visions showed the survivors of Atlantis engaging in the manipulation of strange forces that the old stones had been designed to contain or transmit (see Chapter 6).

Another antiquarian strand that developed in the early years of the 20th century was 'archaeoastronomy' – the modern, scientific study of ancient astronomy (see Chapter 3). A seminal figure in this movement was Sir Norman Lockyer, a respected scientist of his day. After he had discovered astronomical orientations in Greek and Egyptian temples, Lockyer turned his attention to British megalithic sites, partly because he had been impressed by Edward Williams's Gorsedd circle. He visited the Cornish circle of Boscowen-un, which has 19 stones and a leaning central pillar, and identified it as the true prehistoric precursor of Williams's Welsh Gorsedd circle.

Yet a further brand of antiquarianism arose in the years between the two world wars – ley hunting. This was initiated by Alfred Watkins, who believed he had identified on maps and in the field alignments of ancient sites stretching straight across the British countryside (see Chapter 8). He thought these straight lines of sites were the remnants of 'old straight tracks' that had been originally laid down in prehistoric times by line-of-sight surveying methods, which accounted for the straightness. For a number of years, he used an old Anglo-Saxon word, 'ley', as a general name for these alignments, but later he preferred to call them 'archaic tracks' or 'old straight tracks' instead. Watkins published his findings and created considerable interest; a Straight Track Club was formed, and people visited the old monuments and pored over maps, hunting for leys. Similar ideas circulated in Germany and France.

Over this same period dowsing (or water-divining) enjoyed renewed popularity. This is an activity in which a springy twig or other implement appears to move when the person holding it passes over underground water or what-ever else he or she is looking for. The use of dowsing for seeking metal ores by German and Hungarian miners appeared in the literature of the 16th century, while in the 17th century, the antiquarian John Aubrey reported that in Wiltshire 'water may be found by a divining rod made of willowe . . .'. It was clearly a traditional method of finding such things. In the late 19th century dowsing became associated with enquiries into the properties of electricity. A new dowsing tool, the pendulum, made its appearance at this time. This had its origins in spiritualism, where it was used as a method for obtaining 'yes' or 'no' answers to questions directed at spirits.

German dowsers proclaimed that there were noxious influences over certain spots, and 'geopathological' dowsing began to develop. Geopathology relates to various forces from the Earth which cause illness in people affected by them. Some Germans and later others claimed to be able to dowse these forces. Various German dowsers also went on to insist that there were dowsable grids over the Earth's surface, though the size and pattern of these grids varied from one claimant to another! Some French dowsers announced that prehistoric standing stones were located over the crossing of subterranean streams. This was eventually picked up by British dowsers, especially Guy Underwood, who proceeded to develop a complex theory which involved underground streams beneath megalithic sites and early churches. He felt that 'water divining was part of prehistoric religions'. After the death of Alfred Watkins in 1935, leys became associated with both occult 'lines of force' and with dowsing.

There was a renewed interest in the idea of Atlantis after World War Two. The 'sleeping prophet', Edgar Cayce – the American clairvoyant and faith-healer who died in 1945 – claimed that the Atlantean civilisation had been at least the technological equal of our own, and that it had finally blown itself up. He prophesied that part of Atlantis would rise again in the latter years of the 20th century.

'Flying saucers' also made their appearance after the war, and a significant body of opinion in the early days of 'UFOlogy' latched on to the 'hollow Earth' notion, originally put forward in the 19th century. According to this, the Earth was hollow, and contained habitable regions within. The flying saucer enthusiasts of the 1940s and 1950s proposed that the mysterious flying disks entered our world through holes at the poles, and disappeared back through them. In this scenario, the UFOnauts are not extraterrestrials but people from a land inside the Earth, perhaps survivors of

Atlantis. A variant of this belief was that the Atlanteans had been extraterrestrial themselves, and that the flying saucers now seen in our skies derived from Atlantean technology. In short, the extraterrestrial idea was a renewing of the older Atlantis belief – the two motifs became interchangeable.

After World War Two, though dowsing gained in popularity and was used to support ever more ambitious claims, ley hunting virtually faded from view. Atlantean aficionados such as Egerton Sykes in Britain, kept the germ of the ley theory alive through the 1950s, but it was not to come to general attention again until the next decade.

The Swinging Sixties

The psychedelic Sixties saw the explosion of antiquarianism, occultism, and UFOlogy that had been building up over the previous centuries. They were woven into a garish, multi-coloured tapestry that became known as the New Age movement. Leys came back into fashion because they were seen as being lines of dowsable energy that UFOs used to power their motors, while ideas such as Stonehenge having been built to look like a flying saucer were bandied about. Large numbers of people believed they could dowse strange forces at prehistoric monuments and along the 'ley lines' as they had started to be called. 'Vibing' at the old stones became a cool thing to do – or at least to talk about.

Several authors, Erich von Däniken being one of them, claimed that the gods of the ancient world had been astronauts, and that the pyramids, the Nazca lines, the great stone structures of the Americas and the Near East, and the megaliths of Europe had been erected by them, or by humans who had been taught their technology. The new wave of Sixties antiquarians began to seek out further obscure literature, such as early writings on the ancient Chinese system of land-scape divination known as 'feng shui'. (Thirty years later this has become popularised, but back in the hazy days of the 1960s only a relatively small number of Westerners, the ancient sites enthusiasts, knew about it.) Erudite mavericks such as John Michell poured esoteric scholarship into the mix with their books, magazine articles, and self-published book-lets and pamphlets.

This crazy cocktail of latter-day antiquarian beliefs coin-cided with a crisis in archaeology. It was found that the radiocarbon dating system archaeology had been relying on had to be corrected by recalibrating it against the record of tree-ring dating; this had the effect of making old monu-ments even older than had been thought. This trauma was compounded by challenges from scholars outside archaeology indicating that the megalith builders of western Europe and ancient societies elsewhere had possessed sophisticated astro-nomical skills, and by the breakdown of neat theories like diffusionism which had purported to explain the circulation of technical knowledge and social developments through the ancient world. These errors and uncertainties in orthodox prehistory provided a fertile ground for the planting of unorthodox antiquarian ideas in the popular mind.

At the Millennium

The antiquarians of the Sixties needed a convenient label for the heady brew of subjects that together formed their area of interest. Some chose the term 'geomancy' ('earth divina-tion') because it had been used by Victorian writers to describe the landscape art of feng shui, but it wasn't ideal as, strictly speaking, the term refers to the specific practice of casting soil particles for divinatory purposes. Eventually, the term settled upon was 'Earth Mysteries', or, even more blandly, 'ancient mysteries'.

In the popular mind today, Earth Mysteries denotes subjects and ideas such as ley lines, lost civilisations, ancient astronauts, energy dowsing, planetary grids, crop circles, and the use of instruments to measure energies at ancient sites. In reality, though, there is another side to Earth Mysteries. This involves more learned investigations into the astronomical and cosmological aspects of ancient sacred places around the world, the layout of ceremonial landscapes and other aspects of sacred geography, and the ancient mind generally – how it perceived the world, how trance-centred religious activities such as shamanism may have created whole classes of monuments, and so forth. This more mature work – which is often at odds with the New Age version of Earth Mysteries – at times blends with the enlightened trends in modern archaeology, in particular 'cognitive archaeology' mentioned in the Introduction.

So there are really two faces to Earth Mysteries: a popular one displaying New Age beliefs and ideas, and a lesser-known area of original thought and research. The Earth Mysteries situation at the end of the millennium is therefore somewhat schizophrenic in nature.

The Screen of the Past

It can be seen that the folklore of ancient places and the centuries of antiquarianism, the 'backward-looking curiosity', gave rise to a litter of offspring that included not only Earth Mysteries, but also archaeoastronomy, and the discipline of archaeology itself.

It is also apparent that whether in the context of folklore, antiquarianism, archaeology or Earth Mysteries, the

European mind has tended to project its dreams and ideas on to ancient sacred monuments. They have in effect become a kind of screen on to which we all project our pet theories. The challenge is to separate those that are simply modern egotistical fantasies from those that may yield a truth about the ancient mind, which held properties alien to our ways of thinking today. That is the real value of Earth Mysteries – to try to obtain unfamiliar perspectives so we can see ourselves and our world with a fresh vision, and hopefully to reconnect with elements of ancient understanding that we have forgotten or overlooked in our mad, modern rush.

2

The Call of the Old Places

The foundations of the interest in Earth Mysteries are the ancient sacred sites themselves. They call to us from the wild places of the Earth, and from the depths of time, confronting us like half-forgotten dreams. They tantalise us with their mystery, and provoke our imagination, telling of a former world that contained different ways of thinking and being. It may be during a brief visit to picturesque temple ruins while on holiday, or in an encounter with a gaunt standing stone when rambling on a windswept moor, but if the old places call to you, my advice is that you would do well to listen.

Sacred Places of the Earth

The immediate questions that confront the sacred site seeker include: what are ancient sacred sites, what forms do they come in, and where are they to be found? The simple answer is that there are many kinds, and they can be found scattered all over the planet, often, though not always, in the more remote, out-of-the-way places. The Native American image is that sacred places on the Earth are scattered like the spots on a fawn.

To make a generalised study of the evolution of sacred places, we have to start with sites that were considered as naturally holy and preceded monument building: the peaks of a hill or mountain – close to the sky, dwelling places of the gods; a craggy cliff, startling pinnacle or outcrop of rock – perhaps one that looks like a face, or a human or totemic animal figure; a great tree, venerable with age – the rustling of its leaves in the wind sounding like the whispers of invisible beings, triggering visions and prophecies; a roaring waterfall – a chorus of spirit voices calling out of its spray; a cave – entrance to the underworld, the dark womb of the Earth. Sometimes, though, the sanctity ancient people saw in a place is too subtle for our perceptions. In Madagascar, for instance, there is a patch of ground that is known to have been once venerated only because of its old name, which translates as 'There Where One Must Not Spit'!

Such natural places of sanctity may have figured in the tribal myths, or were thought to have a resident spirit or deity, or were simply recognised as having a special aura about them that spoke of the holy. People would repair to such places to have sacred dreams, to fast and undergo a vision quest, to lay offerings, to chant, dance and tell the tribal myths. Certain peoples, such as the Australian Aborigines or various South American tribes, still relate to sacred places in this direct way, but what happened in most cases is that embellishments were made: a few rocks piled up to make a cairn (stone mound), or arranged in a low wall around some dramatic outcrop; a carved post would be erected, or markings engraved into rocks. The first hints of monumentalisation.

As the ages passed, some societies developed agriculture and animal husbandry, and became more settled, slowly losing the old nomadic, hunter-gatherer ways. The people of such societies began to build full-scale monuments, and what we might call sacred architecture began to develop: great timber posts or large standing stones were erected into circles, enclosures, rows and alignments, or used as solitary markers. Stone structures were built in many parts of the world, particularly on the western fringes of Europe and Scandinavia, and in the Mediterranean area. Some megalithic monuments seem to have been designed to imitate natural features, so the interiors of the box-like dolmens of France and Britain, or the so-called passage graves of Newgrange in Ireland, Gavrinis in Brittany, or Antequara in Spain, are reminiscent of caves. In some cases, stone passages and chambers were built underground, or even carved out of the bedrock itself, as was the Hypogeum at Hal-Saflini on Malta.

Stones used in monuments might be left rough, or shaped and smoothed as at Stonehenge; while sometimes other materials would be used for the same purpose as stones – on Yttygran Island near the Bering Strait, for instance, a prehistoric ceremonial complex was constructed of bowhead whale

Chûn Quoit, a typical dolmen

skulls and jaw bones! In various cultures, whole complexes of sacred sites developed, forming extensive sacred landscapes. Indeed, some types of monument were specifically designed as landscape-scale features, so we have strings of earthen effigies, like the effigy mounds of the northern Midwest states of the USA, or giant markings made directly on desert surfaces, such as the Nazca lines in Peru.

In societies that became more complex, with hierarchical social tiers, monument building became even more elaborate, because such societies had developed organisational capacity, and labour was more widely available than in smaller tribes. Such elaborate constructions include not only mighty features like the pyramids of Egypt and the Americas, or great temples such as Borobodur on Java, Indonesia, but whole sacred cities. In Mexico, for instance, there is the ceremonial city of Teotihuacan, built by an unknown people about 2,000 years ago, that even the later Aztecs called the 'birthplace of the gods'. This place started as a ceremonial cave, whose entrance happened to face a significant astronomical direction. Later, a great, stepped pyramid was placed over it, oriented to the same direction, then streets laid out around this with their grid adhering to the same orientation – even streams were canalled to maintain the correct angles. More temples and pyramids were subsequently built within this sacred gridwork. Similarly, in India, the ground plan of the holy Hindu city of Vijayanagara was laid out as a huge representation of the traditional meditation device known as a mandala. Here, temples and architectural features were aligned to indicate key heavenly bodies, such as the Pole Star, or holy hilltops in the local region.

Skills grew with such ambitious projects, especially the ability to work in stone, and the masonry quality of some ancient structures could probably not be matched today. The precision with which huge blocks of stone were fitted together has caused some people to speculate that we are seeing evidence of extraterrestrial or Atlantean technology. These speculators hijack human heritage and degrade human genius, even exporting it off the planet altogether and claiming it originated on extraterrestrial worlds. However, if we deny the human past, we deny our own DNA, our own human spirit. The simple truth is that human genius can flower when and as it is needed. We no longer need those skills on the scale and precision that the ancient societies required, nor do we have the same monumentalising obsession that inspired these cultures (or not in the same way, at least). We have different aims and requirements, and different technologies, hence the skills decline and fall dormant. We can see this even today – how many people do you know who could fashion a wooden cartwheel? Yet only a century ago such a skill was relatively commonplace.

Seasons of the Spirit

The various types of sacred place to a large extent reflect the religious beliefs of the people who used them or built them, and these beliefs have changed in character over time. In remotest antiquity, all people started out with animism and totemism, a form of spirituality associated with tribal societies. In animism, the natural world is seen for what is is: alive, a living world, populated by spirits and spiritual forces. In totemism, animals are seen as being older and wiser than humanity, and certain creatures are thought of as being the spiritual ancestors of specific tribal clans. An 'animal master', the spirit of a species, is conceptualised; people of a bear clan, for example, would address the species spirit of the bear. Permission would have to be sought from it before killing a totemic animal, and in some societies this was forbidden. Totemic and animistic societies tended not to build monuments, but rather to recognise and resort to natural sacred places.

Shamanism emerged from this background. Shamans were inspired prophets and healers, charismatic religious figures who had the power to control spirits and the capacity to enter trance and experience out-of-body 'spirit flight'. The shaman has been described as the 'technician of the sacred'. The shaman was (and still is in some surviving tribal societies) the person who acted as an intermediary between the tribe and the otherworld of spirits. A shaman may heal sick tribal members by locating their lost souls, perhaps entering the otherworld to reclaim them, or by deflecting bad spirits and invisible influences. The shaman was also considered to be able to accompany the souls of dying tribal members into the spirit world, or, again, he or she may travel there to seek information or gain prophetic insight from the spirits. Another role of the shaman was to protect the tribe from the malevolent actions of rival shamans in other tribes, so the shaman had to be proficient in using sorcery as both a defensive and offensive tool: 'shamanic wars' were facts of life in many tribal societies.

Shamans have employed many techniques to attain trance states, including drumming, dancing, chanting, fasting, hyperventilation (rapid shallow breathing), and the taking of hallucinogenic substances; quite often, there was a mix of such methods. In addition, the shaman usually tended to be a person who by nature could easily shift into other mental realities, perhaps as a result of what we would consider to be prevailing medical or psychological condition, or as a consequence of some trauma in childhood or in initiation. Modern psychology describes such people as 'dissociative personalities'.

Strictly speaking, the term 'shamanism' should apply only to its occurrence among Siberian and Central Asian tribes, for it derives from a Siberian tribal word, *saman*. In practice, however, the term is now used widely, even by anthropologists, to describe healers and practitioners anywhere in the world who use ecstatic soul-flight in trance as part of their process. Shamanism is one of the oldest and most universal expressions of human spirituality.

Shamanic societies at the simple tribal level tended not to create monumentalised sacred sites, but there was a stage of development where shamans became chieftains, or where a group of shamanic priests, a 'theocracy', ruled the society. It is now becoming clear that these types of societies *did* build monuments, and of a particularly mysterious kind. Examples include the 3,000-year-old temple of Chavin de Huantar high in the Peruvian Andes, and huge landscape features such as the Nazca lines, or the earthen effigy mounds mentioned earlier. We will look more closely at these 'shamanic landscapes' in Chapter 7.

Societies usually changed in nature when shamans transformed into priests. Priests might or might not be shamanic; where they were not, it meant that they no longer entered trance and the ecstatic state, and so no longer practised the 'hands on' spirituality of the shaman, though they would often maintain shamanistic trappings and display magical abilities. Priest-ruled societies tended to have the qualities of states rather than tribes, and were highly organised, usually warlike, and frequently repressive. A classic case of this transformation occurred with the ancient Maya, who emerged from shamanic, rainforest tribes and developed into a hierarchical, priestly state based on cities, then collapsed back into forest tribes, finally reverting to shamanism which is still carried on to this day.

In certain instances, kingship emerged out of the priestly role, or the two roles would be combined. In the King Arthur myth, for instance, we have the image of a magician or wise man attached to the court in the figure of Merlin, and the belief persisted until recent centuries that British kings and queens had a magic power enabling them to heal by touch. This was a distant echo of the remote shamanic origins of monarchy.

Finally, large-scale and even global religions developed along with statehood, notable examples being Buddhism, Judaism, Christianity, and Islam. These types of religion tend to try to convert other cultures which are usually seen as being 'heathen', adhering to indigenous religious beliefs. Sometimes this is done by missionary persuasion, but often it is accomplished through violence, the European conquest of the Americas being a classic case in point. What becomes lost in this religious form of imperialism is the link between a people and the deities and spirits of their native land. The spirit of place is evicted and replaced by a remote god, usually an 'off Earth' deity, living in or beyond the sky. The temples, mosques, and churches of the big religions were often placed over the earlier holy places as a way of appropriating them. Nevertheless, some of these places evoke considerable sacred power in their own right – for example the Gothic cathedrals of Europe.

None of this is to say that there has been just one tidy stream of religious evolution. Certain societies or cultures remained animistic, totemistic or shamanistic. Some still survive today, though they are marginalised and their ways of life are threatened, if not by the ideological pressures applied to them by the large religions, then by national or corporate predators who feel they stand in the way of the exploitation of natural resources. The ancient knowledge and world-views held by these surviving peoples is what I have called an 'archaic whisper', that is gradually but remorselessly being silenced. Soon, we will be alone in a world where we can hear only our own noise; there will be no promptings from an earlier, and in some cases wiser, world. All the more reason why it is important to reconnect with the old sacred places now, while they can still teach us something.

Answering the Call

Making a conscious, deliberate connection with sacred places is very important for anyone attempting to understand Earth Mysteries. Studying one or two sites in depth can often be better than lightly touching on a lot, but it requires effort. To begin with, you will need to read up on sites to assess the types you are most strongly drawn to. This means visiting bookshops, libraries, and even surfing the Internet if you are able to. When you have settled on a site or two to 'adopt' or develop your own special relationship with, you will need to use a mix of your abilities in order to build up a rounded understanding of it. An ancient – and especially a prehistoric – sacred site is best treated as a *system*, and more specifically an information system that must be accessed in different ways using your intellect, your perceptions on visits to the place, and your intuitive faculties; remember, Earth Mysteries research is multi-disciplinary and multi-mode. Only in this way can the place tell you its full story – and in the process tell you much about yourself.

Let us take a classic monument like Stonehenge as an example, and treat it as a system of knowledge. The hallmark of this monument is its outer ring of stones with lintels, but the *archaeology* of the place tells us that the outer ring is one of the more recent parts of the monument. It didn't start like that. Around 3300 BC, the site was marked by a large wooden building. Then, 100 years or so later, some strange pits and a circular, banked ditch was dug — the actual henge. A few stones were placed in and around the henge, including the outlying giant monolith called the Heel Stone. After about 1,000 years, some more stones were placed in and around the henge, including the famous bluestones, which are the smallest stones seen at the site today. These originated in South Wales, about 200 miles away. A few centuries later, around 2000 BC, an approach avenue from the north-east was built, and local rocks — the sarsen stones — were added. These were smoothed and shaped to make the famous outer, lintel ring, and five massive free-standing trilithons — each consisting of two uprights with a lintel laid across the top — were arranged in a horseshoe-like setting, replacing the bluestones which disappeared for a time. These later reappeared and were placed in a series of settings within the lintel ring. A few other stones were added. The Avenue was added to, and there were alterations and modifications at the site over several following centuries. What we see at Stonehenge today is the end of a long process.

Stonehenge has also taught us much about *ancient astronomy*. We now know that Stonehenge was originally a lunar temple, but during the course of its evolution its axis was changed to point to the midsummer sunrise. A rectangular setting of stones called the Station Stones was set up early in the site's history, and it has been found that it yields many important solar and lunar alignments between its stones. It was also found that when an observer stands in the centre of the henge and looks out through the narrow gaps in the trilithon uprights towards the wider gaps of the outer, lintel

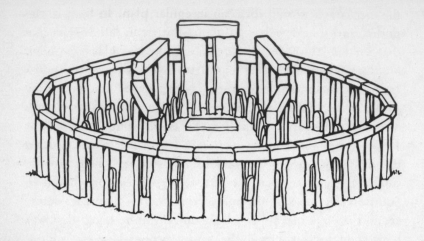

Reconstruction drawing of Stonehenge

circle, astronomically significant parts of the horizon are framed.

The entire landscape in which Stonehenge sits had ancient significance; the monument is part of a wider *sacred geography*, one of five henge monuments in the locality. Before Stonehenge was built, a two-mile utterly mysterious linear earthwork known as the Stonehenge Cursus had already been constructed. There are burial mounds on all sides, dating from both Neolithic and Bronze Age periods. For some reason, the people of Stonehenge felt that whole landscape had to be sanctified.

Some researchers claim to see *symbolism* in the *geometry* of the ground plan of Stonehenge, and in numbers and measures seemingly incorporated into its structure. For example, it has been noted that the four Station Stones form a rectangle because the solar and lunar alignments they mark cross virtually at right angles. This is a function of the monument's latitude, any great distance further north or south, and the

Station Stones would form an irregular plan. In fact, it was discovered that one has to go to the same latitude as that occupied by the Great Pyramid in Egypt to be able to place stones dealing with the same astronomical alignments in a regular pattern. Does this curious coincidence reveal that the builders of Stonehenge knew the dimensions of the Earth? One man who thinks so is one of the founders of modern Earth Mysteries, John Michell. He feels that he has detected ancient units of measurement in the proportions of Stonehenge, and noted geodetic (Earth measuring) symbolism there. An example of this, Michell claims, are the measurements of the outer lintel ring that once ran in a perfect circle supported by the sarsen uprights. These are such that the ring can be seen as a scale model of the Earth's circumference.

Then there is traditional *folklore*. This tells us that the stones of Stonehenge are fossilised giants, that they were brought from Ireland by Merlin's magical arts, and that they can heal – if they are washed with water the collected liquid is said to acquire curative properties.

Finally, there is the *experiential* aspect of the place. A woman was enjoying the solitude of Stonehenge around dawn in 1983, in the days when one could go there without the special permission now required. She suddenly heard a ringing noise she could not account for. Further investigation indicated that the bell-like sounds were actually coming from one of the stones in the north-east quadrant of the henge. The sound stopped as mysteriously as it had begun. An even more dramatic event was experienced by a photographer in the late 1940s, a day before the summer solstice. He knew that on that particular day the sun would be undergoing a partial eclipse as it rose, and he wanted to capture on film the dramatic sight of the sun's partly darkened disk rising up behind the Heel Stone. As he waited patiently for sunrise, there was a loud report, and what he described as a 'ball of fire' hurtled out of the sky and slammed into the ground a few yards away. Lightball phenomena are rare, and to have one occur at Stonehenge, virtually at the solstice and at the time of a partial eclipse, naturally suggests some unusual properties about the site.

In considering a site as complex as Stonehenge, all these factors and more have to be brought together to arrive at as full a sense of the place as possible. In that way, we can get a little closer to the ancient minds that constructed and used it. In the final analysis, that is the purpose of Earth Mysteries involvement – to listen to the archaic whisper.

Your Place

If you were to select a famous site like Stonehenge as 'your' site to study and get close to, you would find any experiential qualities marred by the number of people visiting it, and the problems such intensive tourism brings with it. It is best, therefore, to choose a less well-known, and more isolated site. It could be an old holy well in a Celtic land like Cornwall, Wales, or Scotland, or one of the lesser-known standing stones, stone circles or other monuments on the moors and hills of Britain, Normandy, Brittany, and else-where. It might be a Gothic cathedral visited out of the tourist season, or some forgotten country church; a remote ruin left by the lost Anasazi Indians of the American Southwest, or an earthworked hilltop or ancient burial mound in the many places in Britain and Europe they are to be found. In short, anywhere you can get to at least occasion-ally, avoiding the crowds, and about which you can assemble a range of information.

When you have finally decided on the place (or places) you want to study and interact with, relate to it as you would a wise old teacher. Treat it as if it were living and sentient. This sounds strange, but it will direct your attention in such a way that you might obtain information you might miss in another frame of mind – especially when you are visiting the place. We will discuss this experiential approach further in Chapter 5.

Always respect ancient monuments; do not take parts of them away, mark them, or move them around. Take away only dreams, impressions, photographs, drawings, sounds and smells.

3

Ancient
Skywatching

The use of astronomy at ancient sacred sites is a major Earth
Mysteries theme. On paper, it can appear as a dry, technical
business, but the actual, on-site experience of ancient
astronomy is remarkable. I discovered this many years ago
when some friends and I visited the stone circle of Castlerigg
in Cumbria in the Lake District, in the early hours of a
bitterly cold winter solstice morning (21 December). I had
read *Megalithic Sites in Britain* (1967) by Professor Alexander
Thom, a leading expert on ancient astronomy. He had identified several astronomical alignments at Castlerigg that were
marked by stones opposite one another in the circle. Much of
Thom's book was made up of complex geometry, plans and
equations that quite frankly went over my head, but he had
said that one of the alignments marked the winter solstice
sunrise, so we decided to visit the place and see if he was
right. As the sun burst into view we could immediately see
how two stones formed a distinctive visual connection across
the circle, indicating the sunrise point. The sun's rays felt

warm on our chilled faces, and I felt strangely close to the people who had built and used the site. They too had stood there in the bleak midwinter, had seen the rising sun and felt its warmth, and had made the alignment to it. It was as if I could feel their spirits around us. It was a moving experience, and from that moment on I was hooked on ancient astronomy.

Archaeoastronomy

The origins of archaeoastronomy, the modern study of ancient astronomy, were in folk traditions. In Europe, seasonal fairs and games were often held at ancient sacred places or local landmarks such as prominent hilltops. These festivities often took place at important calendrical times, such as the four solar divisions provided by the solstices and the equinoxes, and the eight solar divisions of the year created when the cross-quarter days are added between – in the old Celtic tradition these were called Imbolc (1 February), Beltane (1 May), Lughnasa (1 August), and Samhain (1 November). The Christian tradition remembers three of these as Candlemas, Lammas, and All Saints. (The May feast of Beltane was not given a place in the Christian calendar, but the May Queen seems to have become associated with the Virgin Mary.) Stonehenge was a classic location for such festivities, and these seasonal events caused antiquarians to start looking for possible astronomical aspects of ancient monuments.

By the turn of the 20th century, ancient astronomy had become a serious topic for many scholars in Germany, France, Ireland and Britain. Sir Norman Lockyer, then editor of the prestigious science journal, *Nature*, discovered that some Greek and Egyptian temples were aligned to the sun or to important stars, and went on to make similar studies of Stonehenge. Taking account of precession (a 'wobble' in the Earth's rotational spin that causes specific rise and set points of heavenly bodies to shift noticeably over long periods of time), he calculated that the axis of Stonehenge had been directed at summer solstice sunrise between 1600 BC and 2000 BC. He also noted that a diagonal across the four Station Stones pointed to certain cross-quarter day sunrises and sunsets. Lockyer's findings were resisted by the archaeologists of his day, but while he did make errors and some dubious claims, ancient astronomy had definitely arrived as a subject worthy of study. Over subsequent decades, a handful of researchers conducted astronomical surveys of prehistoric sites, and with archaeoastronomical work commencing in the 1960s the study was brought to maturity.

Sacred Special Effects

The temple builders of antiquity were consummate showmen, quite capable of using the dramatic impact of astronomical effects. Take the example of the Castillo, a stepped pyramid in the Maya-Toltec ceremonial city of Chichen Itza in Mexico's Yucatan peninsula. Also known as the Temple of Kukulcan, the feathered serpent of Maya mythology and equivalent to the Aztec's Quetzalcoatl, the pyramid is so oriented that an amazing example of shadow-play occurs on the evenings of the equinoxes (21 March and 21 September). As the sun sets, the north-west corner of the pyramid throws a jagged shadow on to the balustrade of a ceremonial stairway on the northern face of the structure. This creates slowly moving triangles of light and shade reminiscent of the markings of the indigenous diamond-back rattlesnake. The top patch of light appears first, and the others show up one at a time until seven triangles of light are strung out down the balustrade, connecting with a carving of Kukulcan's serpentine head at the bottom, thus symbolising the movement of the feathered serpent out of its temple. Because the north face of the pyramid is in shadow at this time, the effect appears all the more dramatic.

Not content with the symbolic use of astronomy, though, it is now thought the builders of the Castillo also made use of acoustics: a curious screeching echo reverberates from the north side of the pyramid in response to any sharp sound like hands clapping, high-pitched chanting, or drumming. Acoustic analysis confirms that this echo is very similar to the call of the Quetzel bird, which was sacred to the Maya. In all, quite a powerful light-and-sound show!

Sun, Moon and Megaliths

The megalithic builders of Europe also knew how to use the astronomical events at their sites for effect. In Aberdeenshire, Scotland, for instance, there are stone circles known as 'recumbent circles' because each of them contains a horizontal, altar-like stone in its periphery. It has been found that to someone standing in one of these circles at specific times in the lunar cycle, the moon appears from behind an upright stone and seemingly rolls across the flat top of the recumbent stone before disappearing behind the next standing stone. It seems the Stone Age ritualists wanted to 'bring down the moon' to their megalithic temples.

The sun could be used in an equally startling way. Examples of this can be found at Loughcrew, in County Meath, Ireland, where several chambered cairns are scattered along a hilly ridge. One of the most prominent of these is called Cairn T. A short passage leads from its entrance into a

Sun-symbol rock carving, Cairn T, Loughcrew, Ireland

main chamber, the back wall of which is decorated with prehistoric rock carvings. Among these are circles surrounded by ray-like markings which look like sun symbols. This was confirmed in the 1980s when it was observed by Earth Mysteries researchers that the rising sun shines into the chamber in the days around the equinoxes. Sunbeams probe into the interior darkness, and because of the angle of the passage and the position of stones within it, the sunlight striking the rock walls is shaped into a rectangular form. As the sun continues to rise, this golden rectangle slides slowly across the back wall of the chamber, finally framing the most complete of the rayed circles. Because there are eight rays, the symbol might represent the eight primary divisions of the solar year.

It is as if the Stone Age people are still communicating with us across the ages.

Star Temples

Lockyer discovered that the Temple of Isis in the Dendera temple complex in Egypt was aligned to Sirius, the brightest star in the sky and associated in Egyptian myth with the goddess. It had further importance to the Egyptians because its first appearance in the dawn skies each year coincided with the annual Nile flood which brought crucial life-giving moisture to the strip of farming land along the length of the great river. Inscriptions on the walls of another temple at Dendera show that it was aligned to the constellation we call the Plough or Big Dipper, and which the Egyptians referred to as the Bull's Foreleg.

Unexplained narrow shafts leading out of the King's Chamber in the Great Pyramid at Giza have also been determined to align to stars. The south shaft is oriented on a star in the constellation of Orion, while the north shaft points towards Thuban, which acted as north or Pole Star for the ancient Egyptians (for us today, the Pole Star is Polaris). In Egyptian mythology, the spirit of the dead pharaoh journeyed to Orion, and to the 'Imperishable Stars' – stars that never sank beneath the horizon at night, like the Pole Star.

In India, the Pole Star figures in the symbolic astronomy of the holy city of Vijayanagara, as mentioned in Chapter 2. When an observer looks north through the great ceremonial gateway on the distinctive north–south axis of Vijayanagara, the gate frames Matangas Hill, on the summit of which stands the Virabhadra Temple. Above that, shines the Pole Star. The builders of the sacred city wanted to link the Temple to the heavens.

Sky Priests of Native America

Many Native American tribes, particularly the Pueblo peoples of the American Southwest, had sunwatcher priests. Hopi sun priests, for instance, would stand on the roof of a certain building in the pueblo and note key agricultural or ceremonial dates by observing the sun's rising and setting positions throughout the year relative to mountain peaks and notches and other horizon features. Other Pueblo Indians had special plates on the interior walls of their adobe homes that marked specific dates when the sun would shine on them through carefully aligned window apertures. One of the main ceremonial centres of the lost Anasazi Indians was Chaco Canyon in New Mexico, where certain rock paintings of sun symbols denote positions where sun priests would have stood 1,000 years ago to observe the progress of the points of sunrise or sunset against specific features on the canyon's rim.

Much further north, near present-day St Louis, are the remains of Cahokia, a vast complex containing Monk's Mound, the tallest prehistoric earthwork in the United States, built by the Mississippi Indians over half a millennium ago. Half a mile to its west, archaeologists also uncovered the post holes of a huge timber ring which they nicknamed 'Woodhenge'. This has been reconstructed and found to have been a sunwatching circle. The priest would stand by a pole near the centre of the circle, and the surrounding ring of posts would mark important sunrise or set positions. The equinoctial rising sun as viewed from the timber circle would appear to be rising out of Monk's Mound, which is where the chief lived. This was powerful symbolism, because European settlers recorded that some Indian chiefs were referred to as 'The Royal Sun' by their tribespeople. The Inca ruler was also known as the 'Son of the Sun', and on the summer solstice he would sit in a gold-sheathed recess in the Coricancha temple in Cuzco, Peru, which glowed and glittered as the rays of the rising sun shone into it.

Sometimes the solar involvement was unusual, as at Simloki (Soldier Mountain) in northern California. At solstitial and equinoctial sunsets, this prominent peak, sacred to the Ajumawi people, throws a shadow that touches various sacred sites in the valley below. In Ajumawi myth, this shadow was considered to be a spirit in its own right and braves would try to outrun it as it spread across the valley floor in order to gain magical power.

In addition to the sun, other heavenly features figured in the skylore of American Indian tribes. The Pleiades constellation was considered important in Central and South America, as at the ancient Mexican city of Teotihuacan, while the planet Venus held great significance for the ancient Maya. A partially ruined tower called the Caracol at Chichen Itza, Mexico, has radiating shafts through its thick walls that align to the extreme northerly and southerly disappearance points of Venus over the western horizon. In Mayan mythology, Venus was associated with warfare and death. Blue was its symbolic colour, and sacrifical victims were sometimes painted blue. The 584-day cycle of Venus was carefully monitored by Mayan priests, and was incorporated into the complex 52-year Mayan ritual and solar calendar system known as the Calendar Round. They also had almanacs recording the cycles of Venus, which were used to identify propitious times for ritual combat and sacrifice; the Great Venus Almanac covered a period of 104 years, which incorporated 65 Venus cycles.

Some Native American astronomy is unusual from a Western perspective. The Aymara Indians of the Andes, for example, have given names to dark patches in the Milky Way, a striking feature of the Andean night sky. These 'dark constellations' are caused by interstellar dust blocking out starlight beyond them.

Chinese Precision

In the 8th century AD, the Chinese erected a series of stone pillars designed to act as gnomons (upright shadow-throwing devices, as on sundials) in a north–south line extending for over 2,000 miles. Over such a distance, the gnomons' shadows varied in length due to the curvature of the Earth's surface. From these variations, the Chinese were able to calculate geographical distances.

In the 13th century AD, the astronomer Guo shou jing built a 40-foot-tall, tower-like device at Gao cheng zhen, south-east of Luoyang. From the north face of this structure there extended a low, water-levelled wall which was called 'The Sky Measuring Scale'. The shadow cast by the tower was marked on the wall at noon on the summer solstice, when the sun was at it highest point in the sky, and again at noon on the winter solstice, when the sun was at its lowest. Measurement of the difference in the lengths of the two shadows enabled Guo shou jing to determine the length of the year with great precision.

Although this precise use of naked-eye astronomy was scientific in a way we can appreciate today, the information was nevertheless used to invest China's imperial rulers with a kind of cosmic authority, because they claimed a heavenly lineage. To be able to pronounce with great accuracy on the calendar and the movements of heavenly bodies confirmed an emperor's celestial credentials in the eyes of the ordinary people.

Making the Cosmic Connection

The sense of time experienced by the former societies that used the kind of skylore we have been looking at was cyclical.

Today we live our lives using a linear sense of time, which we can measure to tiny fractions of a second. Linear time rushes forwards for ever along a single track that disappears into the future, governed by instruments and machines rather than by the cycles of heaven. The ancient sense of time is one of the Earth Mysteries principles we can extract and apply to our modern lives to use as a counterpoint to the stressed-out life-styles most of us are obliged to lead.

EXERCISE: COSMIC RHYTHMS

To develop an awareness of the cosmic rhythms that form the backdrop to our lives, you will need to become, in effect, your own sunwatcher priest or priestess.

☆ Begin by observing where the sun rises and sets relative to features on the skyline around where you live or work, or some place special to you. It doesn't matter if that skyline is made up of hills or mountains, trees or rooftops, factory chimney stacks or a mix of all these. You are simply noting the sun's position against identifiable marker points.

☆ Check the sun's progress every few days, or certainly every week, early in the morning or at sundown, or both. Be particularly observant on the divisions of the old eight-fold year – the solstices, equinoxes, and cross-quarter days mentioned earlier on in this chapter.

☆ You can make a mental note of your 'horizon calendar', or make it more elaborate by taking a series of snapshots of the skyline around you, and pasting these together into a panorama. You can then mark sun positions on that, making a permanent record.

☆ If you live in temperate latitudes, you will not make these observations for many months before you note the astonishing shifts in sunrise and set positions. When I regularly visited the Rollright Stones near Oxford during Dragon Project work at the site (see Chapter 4), I was astounded how much further north the sun rose in summer than in winter.

☆ Mark the position of sunrise or sunset on the skyline on your birthday – that way you will have a visual, temporal, and geographical record of your place in the cosmic scheme of things. Connect your life to the greater rhythms of nature.

4

Places of Power

One of the most persistent Earth Mysteries rumours is that strange forces operate at ancient sacred places – particularly prehistoric megalithic monuments. Again, this somewhat startling and contentious belief has its origins in folklore.

Strange Tales

A number of traditional folklore motifs that relate to prehistoric sites can be identified in Britain and elsewhere. One is that certain standing stones have healing properties, like the holed Men-an-tol in Cornwall, which was believed to cure people of pains in the back and limbs if they crawled through its central hole. Some megaliths were credited with the power to bring down thunder and lightning if anyone interfered with them. The stones in certain circles were said to be uncountable, while others were said to be capable of movement, such as going for a drink at nearby streams, or were people turned to stone for transgressing some taboo. This theme of petrifaction is widespread: for example, a set of standing stones south of Morlaix in Brittany is called An Eured Ven, 'the Wedding Party', a group of people turned to stone because they blocked the way of a priest. The Stanton Drew circles in Somerset, England, are likewise said to be a wedding party turned to stone for allowing revelries to continue into the Sabbath. Exactly the same legend is attached to a stone circle near Kaur, in the Gambia, Africa.

Another piece of lore is that the old stones can promote fertility and fecundity. In Brittany, for instance, women resort to the dolmen of Cruz-Moquen, also known as La Pierre Chaude, and raise their skirts at full moon in the hope of becoming pregnant. Dancing stones is also a fairly common theme. Sites like the Merry Maidens stone circle in Cornwall, or the Nine Maidens circle in Devon, for example, are said to dance, or to have been dancers turned to stone. The stones of St Lythans chambered cairn in South Glamorgan, Wales, are supposed to twirl around three times then bathe in a nearby river!

Other ancient monument lore includes themes involving giants and the Devil (often interchangeable motifs), buried treasure, dragons and divination.

Fairy Lights

An intriguing strand of folklore associates specific sites with fairies or other elemental entities. Quite often, it is unexplained lights that are interpreted as fairies, and it is interesting to note that anecdotal accounts frequently involve lights at sites, as can be deduced from even a brief set of examples. In Shropshire, there is a stump of stone known as the Fairy Stone. Within living memory, a farmer was on his way home one evening when he saw small lights sitting on the grass around the stone. He kicked at them and some stuck to his trouser leg. Somewhat concerned, he knocked them off and rushed homewards. When he arrived there, he noticed that his trousers were holed where the lights had been. In the 19th century, tin miners passing the Ballowall Barrow (Carn Gloose) near Land's End, Cornwall, would occasionally report seeing small lights dancing there. These were assumed to be fairies. Several other locations in Cornwall attracted similar reports. In Ireland, Crillaun, a 'fairy fort' (prehistoric earthwork) in County Mayo, sometimes appeared spangled with small, moving lights. These were naturally thought to be fairies by the locals. In 1919, two hill walkers in the Lake District encountered large balls of white light drifting over the Castlerigg stone circle. They panicked when one of the six-foot-wide globes started floating across the field towards them, but to their great relief it dissolved silently.

It may have been that such phenomena seen at specific locations in ancient times were perceived as spirits or, more generally, as manifestations of the sacred, and caused monuments to be built at them. This certainly happened on the sacred Chinese mountains of Wu Tai shan and Omei shan, for example, where large, floating spheres of golden light have long been seen around their peaks at night and were interpreted as 'Bodhisattva Lights'. A tower was erected at a summit temple on Wu Tai shan specifically for viewing these holy lights. In India, two pilgrimage shrines dedicated to the Goddess Bhagbatti on the Purnagiri Mountains were likewise erected because of local light phenomena. The sacred shrines are situated on a geological fault. While staying at Dilkusha, also in India, the distinguished Tibetan Buddhist, the late Lama Anagarika Govinda, saw mysterious lights in the foothills of the Himalayas. His host told him that the lights were often seen, and he himself had once witnessed them moving through his palace grounds towards a temple. That spot had always been considered a sanctified place, he said.

Fault Lines

The nature of the lights described above is unknown; I call them 'earth lights' for want of a better term. The evidence suggests that they are geophysical, and related to curious lights sometimes produced by earthquakes. They are certainly exotic phenomena, whatever they are.

Their connection with sites may be due to a common factor – geological fault lines. These are cracks in the Earth's surface where tectonic movement such as causes earthquakes and tremors tends to occur more frequently then elsewhere. High concentrations of mineral deposits often occur along fault lines, too, and this can cause electro-magnetic anomalies.

Stone circles and stone chambers in Britain are known to correlate with the distribution of geological faulting. This may have been because stone was more plentiful in such regions, in which case the association may have been purely accidental, or it may have been because lights were seen relatively often in such areas and so they were seen as special or holy. Indeed, there is some evidence to indicate that ancient people did consider faulting as important. For instance, the ancient Icelandic ceremonial centre, the Althing, was deliberately sited in a rift valley, Thingvellir, by the Scandinavian settlers, while in Arizona, the Indians who built the ancient Wupatki pueblo complex recognised the great fault system lying beneath them by incorporating the associated 'blow holes' into their structures. (These blow holes 'breathe' the great volumes of air circulating within the subterranean fault system in and out in alternating six-hour periods.)

The founding myth of the great Greek oracle site of Delphi tells of a goatherder who, overcome by fumes issuing from a crevice in the ground, went into a prophetic trance. The later prophetesses at the Temple of Apollo built at the site were said to sit on a special stool over the fissure in order to breathe in the mind-changing fumes. Although most scholars have dismissed this as pure legend, recent scientific work has in fact confirmed the presence of faulting beneath the Temple.

Experiences at Sites

Many Earth Mysteries followers consider that folklore associating ancient sites with unusual powers and strange properties represents garbled memories of weird experiences at such places in generations past. Although folklorists would say that there are many other explanations for the various folklore motifs, there may be something in this argument, for there have been a number of anecdotal accounts of odd happenings in modern times.

A researcher at the Newgrange chambered mound in Ireland told me that early one morning, as he entered the passage leading to the central chamber, he lazily touched the lintel stone over the entrance. He received a powerful shock, like a discharge of static electricity. A member of the National Trust similarly told me that when he touched one of the stones in the King's Men circle at Rollright, he received an electric-like shock that numbed his forearm for 20 minutes.

In *Places of Power* (1990, 1999), I recount the experience of a local government worker who was strolling around the

Cumbrian stone circle of Long Meg and Her Daughters, when he went into an unusual trance-like state when passing stones in the site's north-west quadrant. In another example, an archaeologist told me of unusual flickering lights he saw on the underside of the capstone at the Chûn Quoit dolmen, Cornwall, when he was investigating the interior of the monument.

There are many other such reports of people feeling shocks, seeing odd lights or feeling strange at ancient monuments. Many could simply be imaginary, but in some cases, it seems possible there was an objective component too – though that doesn't mean it has to be supernatural or inexplicable.

The Dragon Project

Shortly after taking over editorship of The Ley Hunter in 1976, I invited papers for an issue of the journal to be dedicated to the question of 'site energies'. The response was disappointing. A few people wrote in with their thoughts and opinions, but there was no first-hand research. So in 1977, in an attempt to determine what substance, if any, there was to the topic, I organised a meeting for all those interested in setting up a project to research the matter. Physicists, dowsers, chemists, electronic engineers and people simply interested in the idea turned up, and a lively evening ensued. It resulted in the setting up of the Dragon Project, named after the Chinese symbol for Earth forces. This was a part-time effort with a shifting flux of volunteers, and very limited funding. The Project was allowed to make use of the Rollright Stones – a site with one of the richest bodies of folklore attached to it – as a fieldbase.

The Dragon Project began work in 1978, focusing mainly on physical, measurable energies, although some on-site testing using psychics and dowsers was also attempted. The sites monitored included British prehistoric monuments in the main, but a few sessions were also conducted at sites in France, Greece, Egypt and the United States. Project members started out by searching for measurable energies that might be expected to be present at megalithic monuments, linking these where possible to reports of people's unusual experiences at those places.

Radioactivity was an early research target – not the sort associated with nuclear power stations, but natural background radiation caused by emissions from rocks, especially granite, and from the sky as a result of cosmic ray bombardment of the upper atmosphere. The Dragon Project wanted to see if there were anomalies in this low-level background buzz of radiation around prehistoric monuments. This entailed a great deal of environmental radiation monitoring before there was any hope of identifying anomalies, but it gradually became apparent that some standing stones did emit unusual amounts of gamma radiation. The Long Meg and Her Daughters stone circle in Cumbria, England, was measured because of the anecdote recounted above, and research indicated that the stones in the north-west quadrant of the stone circle had localised areas on them emitting constant streams of radiation, much stronger than the levels recorded on the surfaces of the other granite stones. Could this somehow have affected the man's mental state?

In addition to this type of anomaly, the Dragon Project encountered heightened natural radiation in other sacred site contexts. The waters of numerous healing wells and springs, for instance, proved to be radioactive. A notable example was found at the famous hot springs of Bath, in Somerset, England. These were in use at least 7,000 years ago, and later, in the Iron Age, became a Celtic shrine. The Romans then turned it into a temple and bathing complex, and it was still a renowned spa well over a millennium later, in Georgian times. The thermal waters rising at Bath have been found to contain appreciable amounts of radium, and when the Dragon Project monitored water issuing from an old Roman arch beneath the Great Bath, a significant level of natural radioactivity was confirmed. The Project further discovered that quite a range of Celtic holy wells also produced mildly radioactive water.

Heightened radiation levels were also measured inside Neolithic and Iron Age stone chambers. This was because they are enclosed granite structures. Interestingly, during a visit to Egypt I found that the interior of the King's Chamber inside the Great Pyramid yielded virtually identical radiation counts to these British monuments. Although the Great Pyramid is constructed from limestone, the King's Chamber is clad in Aswan granite, a stone the ancient Egyptians associated with 'spirit'.

Magnetism occurring naturally was another energy possibility researched by the Dragon Project, and two forms of magnetic anomaly were noted at ancient sacred places. The first consisted of low-level magnetic fluctuations in standing stones, measurable only with sensitive magnetometers. These fluctuations could last for up to one or two hours, and then the stone would revert to normal. The Project was unable to carry out a sufficiently comprehensive survey to find out just how common this effect was, though indications were that it was occasional and apparently random. The cause of the fluctuations was not discovered. The other magnetic effect was more dramatic: it was found that some stones at megalithic sites could deflect a compass needle held near them. This effect is due to iron content in the stones having a field 'set' when the rock was formed that is at variance with today's geomagnetic field. Although there is nothing inherently mysterious about this, members of the Dragon Project felt that the presence of such stones at specific sites could possibly be of significance.

The Project also uncovered other apparent anomalies at ancient sites, such as cloud-like shapes recorded on infra-red film, and unexplained ultrasound activity, particularly around sunrise, but there were difficulties evaluating these and other odd effects.

Since the Project's physical monitoring programme came to an end in the early 1990s, a few other researchers have conducted similar investigations. A wider survey of sites for magnetic effects has been conducted, but no clear pattern has emerged. In America, a scientist has uncovered indications that a recurring symbol found in prehistoric Native American rock art in Arizona and Nevada may indicate locations of strong natural radioactivity – so strong, indeed, that she had to undergo decontamination procedures when she returned home from one of the sites involved.

The Ancient Sensing of Earth Energies

There is the question of whether the megalith builders and other early peoples could have sensed energies like magnetism and radiation. Regarding magnetism, it is possible that it could have been detected by magnetite (lodestone), or even directly by the human organism. In 1992, scientists at the California Institute of Technology in Pasadena found that tiny deposits of magnetite existed in all human tissues, especially brain cells. This explains why the human brain can be very sensitive to changes in magnetic fields, and research shows that this can trigger hallucinatory or visionary episodes in some people. It is not unreasonable to suspect that people long ago knew the subtleties of their geophysical surroundings as surely as we now know they did their living, botanical environment. While our magnetic sensitivities are dulled by the maelstrom of electromagnetic fields to which we are subjected, theirs would have been fresh and sharp. Further, Professor Michael Persinger at Laurentian University in Ontario, Canada, has found that factors such as diet may have made the prehistoric builders and users of the sites particularly sensitive to ambient magnetic fields. In particular, lack of certain nutrients could affect foetal development, resulting in individuals with slight changes in their brain structure, rendering them more liable to visionary and psychic experiences.

Although people long ago naturally did not use Geiger counters, and it is currently supposed that human beings cannot directly sense radioactivity, some laboratory experiments have shown that simple organisms do react to radiation. Also, prolonged exposure to places harbouring a certain type of radioactive material could result in certain recognisable physical conditions. Ancient peoples would come to regard locations like this as being haunted by powerful − and even dangerous − spirits.

How Earth Energies May Have Been Used

In the ancient world there would not have been talk of magnetism, of course, but stones with what we would identify as magnetic properties would doubtless have been considered magical objects or 'spirit stones' that could facilitate contact with the supernatural world, or cause visionary states. This would especially be the case if a person was already in a sensitised state by means of dancing, drumming, and other ritual activities.

Places of heightened background radiation may have been sought for healing purposes, in particular some holy wells. It has long been suggested that radiation in limited doses can have a homeopathic-style beneficial effect; a century ago people resorted to radioactive caves in Colorado in the way others went to spas. Even today, some sick people allow themselves to be exposed for timed periods to the heightened radiation in old uranium mines in Montana, and remarkable cures have been claimed.

The Dragon Project became convinced that areas of heightened background radiation could also trigger visionary experience, because some of its volunteers reported brief but intense visionary or hallucinatory mind states in such locations. So, long ago, places like this may have been regarded as places of vision.

EXERCISE: DETECTING SITE ENERGIES

You don't have to be a scientist or a technical whiz-kid to try out simple forms of energy detection at sites.

☆ Obtain a liquid-filled compass such as can be bought for a modest price from outdoor sports shops, or Army and Navy-type stores. (Liquid-filled compasses are best because the liquid slows down the movement of the compass needle, whereas the needle in dry compasses flickers and moves too much to be useful for detection purposes.)

☆ Next, set off to explore an old monument or a place that the ancients considered to be a place of power. I give a gazetteer of British 'magnetic monuments' in my book *Places of Power*, but you can try out your compass at any megalithic site you visit.

☆ Pass it over the surface of the stones, but without touching them. Make the action smooth and steady, keeping the face of the compass horizontal. It will take a little practice, so start off with slow and careful actions. You will soon be able to identify any magnetic anomalies on a standing stone – the needle will spin in a distinctive manner.

You can also use this method at natural sacred places. For example, it was found that the rocks on the top of Carn Ingli ('Hill of Angels') in the Preseli hills in Pembrokeshire (where the Stonehenge bluestones came from) were highly magnetic; sometimes, the compass needle would point fully south instead of north. Carn Ingli was where the 6th-century holy man, St Brynach, went to fast and meditate, and where he saw visions of angels: a holy peak. Similarly, I was shown a Native American 'power spot' on Mount Tamalpais above San Francisco. It was an outcrop of green serpentine, and I discovered that a compass needle went wild at a certain point on it. You could sit there, overlooking the Pacific Ocean, with your spine in this anomalous magnetic field and your head in the normal magnetic field of the Earth. For someone meditating over a long period, or fasting and engaged in a vision quest, the variations in the magnetic fields could quite possibly help promote visionary mental states.

There is no limit to instrumental detection for the technically minded – it is easy enough to purchase a cheap or second-hand Geiger counter, for example. But there really is no need, unless you want to make it a special part of your Earth Mysteries involvement; just to see a magnetic needle moving in an unusual way at a site is enough to make you realise that there really are energies at some sacred places. There is nothing supernatural about it, but it does suggest that some sacred sites may have been designed to use natural energy to enhance their power in provoking mental states of the spiritual or visionary kind. If you identify such a spot, it would be worthwhile using it as a place to meditate or conduct your inner work, or even to sleep – there was a whole ancient tradition of 'temple sleep'.

It must always be borne in mind, though, that the fact that energy anomalies have been measured at ancient holy sites does not prove that they were deliberately sought out, or even known about, by the original users of those places. It is all down to interpretation.

5

Mind, Body and Sacred Space

Ancient monuments can be places of power in a deeper sense than simply displaying energy anomalies; they can exert strong psychological and even spiritual effects on a person visiting them. To deal with this aspect of Earth Mysteries requires the ability to approach a sacred site using the primary awareness of the bodily senses and inner faculties, such as feeling and intuition. These should not replace logical, intellectual methods, but complement them.

Spirit of Place

A sacred place can interact with our mind and feelings in a dynamic way. It contains its own mythic nature, sometimes called *genius loci* or spirit of place. This may not be visible but can be apprehended by humans (and even animals), especially in the appropriate mental state. Indeed, your state of mind will determine exactly how much and what kind of information a holy place can impart to you. It is best if you treat such a placc as if it were a wise old person, like a venerable teacher.

On a less esoteric level, the forms, textures, smells, sounds or lights of a particular place can trigger associations within us that another place would not. It can bring things into awareness that until then existed only in the unconscious mind. Sacred places can therefore illuminate us. In his book, *Placeways* (1988), the American writer and researcher Eugene Walter suggests that we try to appreciate any special place as somewhere that 'evokes and organises memories, images, feelings, sentiments, meanings, and the work of the imagination'. It is good advice.

The Nature of Sacred Places

When visiting a sacred site, it is helpful to know – or at least guess – what role it might have been designed to fulfil. Places were considered holy for many reasons – as spirit residences, ceremonial areas, legendary and mythological places, burial sites, sacrificial altars, resource areas for special materials used in ceremony and ritual, or locations for dream divination or for seeking visions. Some sites were seen as transformation places, where journeys to the spirit world could best be undertaken. Mescalero Apaches identified spots specifically for this purpose, and Hindus refer to such places as *tirthas*, meaning 'crossing' or 'fords', hence places to help one cross over into the visionary otherworld of spirit or mind. The religious historian Mircea Eliade similarly considered a sacred place to be one where a breakthrough between the material and spiritual worlds could be expected. He termed such a supernatural occurrence a 'hierophany'.

Many non-Western cultures have recognised a form of non-material power at certain spots, a supernatural potency. The Mescalero call this *diyi*, while other Native Americans refer to it as *Po-wa-ha* (Pueblo), *orenda* (Iroquois), *wakonda* (Sioux) and *maxpe* (Crow). The Australian Aborigines have a range of words, including *djang* and *kurunba*; in North Africa it is called *baraka*; the Bushmen of the Kalahari call it *n/um*; in Hindu tradition it is *prana*; and in old Chinese lore it is *ch'i* (or *ki* in Japanese spiritual tradition). Most famously, in the Pacific islands it is known as *mana*. Places, objects and the human body can contain this mystic power. It would be unwise of us to think in terms of 'energies' when considering this ancient cross-cultural concept, and that is why I make a clear distinction between this kind of power and the energies we can measure with instruments, be they compasses, Geiger counters, or even dowsing rods. The traditional terms listed refer to the sense of being at a particular place, or in the case of a person, the aura of dignity or personal holiness.

German theologian Rudolf Otto explored this matter in his book, *The Idea of the Holy* (1924). He considered feelings of eeriness or awe to be the 'earliest manifestation' of the holy. This mental effect can pass away, but sometimes, he noted, it can be articulated through, or by reference to a place. This is how, in Otto's opinion, the concept of the holy place developed. He used the term 'numinous' to describe the haunting quality some sacred places can possess – a *numen loci*. The great psychologist C.G. Jung coined the term 'numinosity' from this, and Freud reported experiencing it when he visited the Acropolis in Athens for the first time as a young man.

Sense of Place

The ancient Greeks had two words for place, *chora* and *topos*. *Chora* was a holistic reference to place, referring to place as a point of experience, as a trigger to memory, imagination and the sense of mythic presence. In his *Timaeus*, Plato claimed that *chora* could not be apprehended by the senses alone, but required a kind of 'special reasoning' and the ability to 'dream with our eyes open'. I think he probably meant this quite literally. I am one of those strange people who occasionally sleeps with eyelids slightly apart, and on a number of occasions I have woken to discover that some object in my dream was based on something my sleep-laden eyes were fixed on in the bedroom – for example, a waving figure in a dream can transform into drapes blowing gently in a breeze coming through an open window. What seems to be happening is that objects seen in the mundane world of waking consciousness acquire a mythic dimension when filtered through dream consciousness. The visionary poet William Blake could see the mythic in the mundane, for he told us that double the vision was always with him, so that a thistle across his way could also appear to him as 'an old man grey'. Such 'mythic consciousness' is a waking form of the dream state, and can be developed in waking consciousness, or cultivated in the dreaming sleep state, when it is called 'lucid dreaming', that is, being consciously awake while in a dream and physiologically asleep. It was the famed scholar of myth and legend, Joseph Campbell, who most aptly equated dream and myth, when he said that myths are public dreams and dreams are private myths.

Topos, on the other hand, signified place in much the way we think of it today – simple location and the objective, physical features of a locale. This sense of place eventually overtook *chora*, the older term, until even sacred places became *topoi*.

These quite different approaches to place exemplify an important turn in the intellectual history of the West. The result is that collectively, at the mainstream level of our modern culture, we have lost the sense of place that *chora* implied. Individually, however, many of us still have responses to place that relate more to *chora* than *topos*, but such feelings about a place are admitted only quietly to friends; in the broader cultural context any discussion of feeling strange at a site, or of being powerfully affected by an ancient holy place, is treated as an amusing, anecdotal matter of no real consequence.

An Holistic Way of Visiting Ancient Sacred Sites

What we think of as tourism, the ancient Greeks called *theoria* (perhaps making them the first 'theorists' rather than tourists). When visiting an unfamiliar place the Greek theorists would ask questions of locals, listen to the stories and myths of the location, and observe, listen to and obtain a 'feel' for the place. Many areas had *periegetes*, guides who could explain the sites, local customs, myths and so on. They were the living repositories of the local lore and knowledge.

What the Greeks called *theoria*, I have elsewhere referred to as 'monumenteering' – the holistic way of experiencing ancient sacred places. A vaguely similar approach was practised in Iceland, Scandinavia and northern Europe in the early part of the historical era, but its origins may reach back into prehistory. It was referred to as 'sitting out', and involved the seer (a shaman-like practitioner of European tradition) entering a trance in order to summon spirits for divination, or going on 'seers' journeys – a clairvoyant exercise, or perhaps a version of the ecstatic soul flight associated with shamanism. In Norway this tradition is recorded in the context of men sitting out on burial mounds in order to receive occult wisdom. In Iceland (and probably elsewhere in

Britain and Europe), seers went to specific, isolated cross-roads at certain dates such as New Year's Eve or the eve of St John's Day (24 June) in order to become entranced and to summon spirits.

Monumenteering is a little less demanding and slightly occult, but can give intriguing new insights into ancient places – and into yourself. It is a way of not only visiting a sacred site physically, but also of engaging with the site at a mythic level, allowing it to provoke memory and unsuspected associations. The first step in monumenteering is to decide on an ancient sacred place to visit, either as a special trip or part of your holiday schedule. There are plenty of books that list and describe sites all over the world, so the first part of your monumenteering journey will be a quick trip to your library or bookshop. Select a site that you have not been to previously. Before you visit it, read all you can about it and study any photographs you can find. Try to imagine the place in your mind's eye.

Next, visit the site, temple or monument. Take a camera or sketch pad with you. Enter the site alone if possible, but if not, then at least wait until there are only a few people around – choose your moment. In that first encounter, try to sense the difference between the place as you experience it and the place as you imagined it before you came. Mentally examine that difference; try to recognise what it is that is different. Is it the size of the monument? The area it encloses? The extent and nature of the surroundings? Whatever the difference, identify it and try to *feel* it. Remember that feeling.

Adjust your mental frame so that you encounter the site as if it was a living, sentient being. I cannot emphasise this enough, for doing this allows the place to tell you its story. It is as if you have tuned your receiver to pick up a specific station. If you think of the site as just a heap of earth or stones, you haven't even switched on your psychospiritual 'radio'.

Conversations with Remarkable Places

In his book, *The Rediscovery of North America* (1990), nature author Barry Lopez writes powerfully of when he visited a desert area of Africa. Local elders taught him how to sit down in one place for two or more hours at a time and look at the landscape around him. We should enter a landscape to learn something, Lopez suggests, and should pay attention rather than constantly posing questions. We should 'approach the land as we would a person, by opening an intelligent conversation'. Lopez promises that if we make such a long and intense observation – 'a fully dilated experience' – we will have an interaction with the environment that is more complex even than language. This will work as much for an ancient holy place as it will for natural surroundings.

In case you think this is simply poetic licence, I offer this account of my own work at Avebury in Wiltshire. Avebury is a complex, which means that it is made up of a whole set of monuments scattered over a 'ceremonial landscape'. The village of Avebury sprawls into the huge, 28-acre henge which contains the world's largest stone circle. Two rows of stone, the Kennet Avenue, run south from the henge. Barely a mile to the south-west of the henge is Silbury Hill, at 130-feet high it is the tallest man-made structure in prehistoric Europe. Scattered among the natural hills and undulations of the landscape are a range of other monuments, notably earthen long barrows, containing stone passages and small chambers. The most famous monument of this type in the complex is the West Kennet long barrow, a chambered

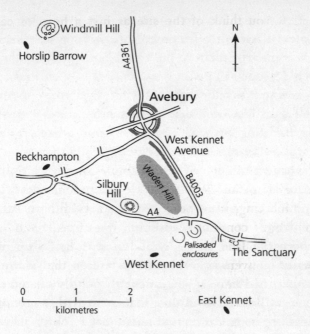

A simplified plan of the Avebury complex

earthen mound some 300 feet in length. Taken together, the Avebury monuments range in age from about 3700 BC to around 2600 BC.

I had been visiting the complex for many years, attempting to understand something about the way the builders of Avebury might have thought, and what their monuments might have meant to them. It all had to be there in this ceremonial landscape, yet I just couldn't get to grips with the meaning of the place. In a moment of frustration, I actually fell on my knees within Kennet Avenue and invoked the spirit of the place out loud, imploring that it help me understand the complex.

There was no sudden revelation. No genie flickered into visibility before my startled gaze. But something different did begin to happen on my subsequent visits to the Avebury complex. I started to become powerfully aware that Silbury Hill was the true focus of the ritual landscape; the hub of the wheel. As soon as I became aware of this, a curious relationship seemed to develop between the great mound and myself. I distinctly felt that it was sentient, and was somehow communicating with me. I also became acutely aware that this was a non-rational way of thinking, so I made it a rule that whenever I entered the Avebury complex I would click fearlessly into this 'mythic' mode of consciousness, but that when I left I would revert to my normal, 20th-century mode of thinking. I began to realise that what had been holding up my perception of this special, ancient landscape was my incessant questioning. Did the sun rise on midsummer's day over there? Is there an alignment through these sites? What happens at Beltane from this, that or the other monument? I was making so much mental noise that I couldn't hear what the place was telling me, much less see it. As soon as I learned to adopt a quieter, passive-alert approach, the situation changed, and at every visit I learned some small piece of information that I could never have predicted.

One day I noticed a subtle, eroded ledge that ran round the otherwise smooth slopes of Silbury Hill about 17 feet down from its flat summit. I found that this was mentioned in archaeological texts, but little commented on. I moved around the whole sacred landscape, looking up periodically at Silbury, which from some angles dominated the landscape, yet from other places disappeared into the folds of the land. Until 1970, Silbury had been assumed by archaeologists to have been Europe's largest Bronze Age burial mound, but excavation showed it to be considerably older (Late Neolithic, around 2700 BC) and there was no central chamber or rich burial. What there was, however, was grass, so remarkably well preserved in the heart of the mound that it was still green. Among it were the intact bodies of flying ants, indicating that work had started on the monument either at the end of July or in the early part of August thousands of years ago. The mystery deepened as to why, then, the ancients had built this great monument, uniquely constructed out of 12 million cubic feet of chalk then covered and smoothed with earth. And people were equally puzzled as to why anyone should have built anything so tall as this mound at the lowest spot in the valley of the little River Kennet and alongside a natural ridge, Waden Hill, of about the same height.

Then, one day, while standing on West Kennet long barrow, Silbury Hill finally got through to me. The communication had been visual all along. I noticed that the distant skyline passed behind Silbury Hill's profile at just the point where the ledge interrupted its smooth sides. I immediately set off to stand at the other monuments that most closely ringed Silbury Hill. From them all, the far horizon appeared to pass behind the profile of the great mound somewhere between its ledge and flat summit. The view of Silbury from within the henge circle at Avebury was particularly dramatic: standing at the site of what had been the tallest stone within the main circle, the same top segment of Silbury between summit and ledge was just visible, rising up in a cleft formed by a dip in the distant horizon and the angle of the lower slope of Waden Hill in the near foreground. But I later found that just before harvest time, when the cereal crop on Waden Hill was at its tallest, this view to Silbury was blocked by the height of the crop. It was a *harvest-dependent sightline*. The significance of this exploded within me like a revelation. Harvest time was July and early August – Lughnasa in the old Celtic calendar, or Lammas in the Christian one – the very period when Silbury had started to be constructed. It became

Silbury Hill showing the eroded ledge

transparently clear to me that Silbury Hill was a huge harvest mound, a representation of the bountiful Earth Mother. I felt that Silbury had actually told me this, revealing an open secret that had been unnoticed for thousands of years.

The next question was why the ancient builders had engineered this curious visual coincidence concerning Silbury and the horizon? I visited Silbury regularly, at all times of the day and night and periods throughout the year, and sat on its flat, platform-like summit, gazing out at the monuments and natural landscape below. Without knowing it at that time, I was, in effect, 'sitting out' like the seers of old. Then, early one morning, I was sitting on Silbury's summit in a quiescent, possibly light trance state, when a voice as clear as a bell spoke into my ear: 'In this mystery shall we dwell'. Startled, I turned my head, knowing even as I did so there would be no one there. It had been what a rationalist would call an auditory hallucination, but to me, there and then, it was as if Silbury itself had actually spoken to me.

A few weeks after this bizarre episode, the mystery was made clear to me. As I witnessed a glorious Beltane sunrise, it became apparent that the eastern horizon viewed from Silbury was 'double', in that the far distant skyline exactly mimicked the contour of the nearby ridge of Waden Hill in the foreground. From Silbury's summit the two skylines were just visually separated, the distant one appearing fractionally above the other. But there was a slight dip in the middle of the span of the distant horizon, and I realised that this meant that if the sun was seen to rise in that dip while viewing from the summit of Silbury, it could be seen to rise a second time shortly afterwards from the ledge 17 feet below, because the slight dip was just obscured by Waden Hill when the viewpoint was lowered to the ledge. This dip in the skyline was where the Lughnasa sun would also rise, for sunrise occurs at the same point on the horizon at both Beltane and Lughnasa. By now, the sun had risen too far to actually test this effect, and I had to wait two more years before I could find the opportunity to witness it. That came about on 1 August 1989, and an archaeologist came to see the event with me. Sure enough, we saw the Lughnasa sun rise over the far horizon, then we immediately slid down the grassy slope to the ledge, where a couple of minutes later the sun's rays broke over the huge bulk of Waden Hill. The height and location of Silbury had been exactly worked out to unite the various monuments round about, the natural lay of the land, and the seasonal movements of the sun.

There was one further revelation. I climbed Silbury the following day to photograph the double-sunrise event. After doing this, I turned to descend the great mound, but a glorious sight stopped me in my tracks. To the west, as the sun rose behind me, the long shadow of Silbury was thrown across the fields. Issuing out of the top of the shadow was a golden light that shimmered across the countryside. My mythical consciousness knew instantly that this magical light was Silbury's — the Earth Mother's — blessing on the land. Later, in rational mode, I discovered that it was an optical effect known as a 'glory', caused by the refraction of sunlight in dewdrops. You can see something similar yourself: if you stand in a field or on a lawn at sunrise with your back to the sun you will see a golden glow around your head, like an aura. The German term for the effect is 'Holy Light'. On Silbury, the spectator's shadow is thrown across the flat top of the mound as far as the shoulders, but the head part of the shadow is cast hundreds of feet below into the main shadow of the mound, causing a greatly enhanced glory effect.

EXERCISE: MONUMENTEERING

The above account indicates the frame of mind in which you should approach your selected site. Listen to what it will tell you. Keep all your mental and sensory channels open.

☆ What are the legends associated with this place? If you know them, run them through your mind as you move around the site.

☆ Look at the surroundings and note how the site relates to its broader environment.

☆ How does the site make you feel? A little fearful, awe-struck, happy, dreamy, or somehow disappointed? Don't analyse these feelings, simply register them.

☆ How does the site smell? There may not be a particular smell that you are readily conscious of, but sometimes there is, especially after rain. I recall visiting the Greek oracle site of Delphi after a torrential storm and being overwhelmed by the scent of freshened earth, and particularly of cypress trees. Now, if I smell cypress a sunlit picture of Delphi flashes before my mind's eye. Smell can powerfully evoke emotion and memory, so if you have the opportunity, visit your selected site either prior to or just after a storm, or during low pressure when there is more moisture in the atmosphere and scents carry more readily. In the evening, too, ambient scents tend to be stronger.

☆ If you can't detect a 'site scent', come prepared with a piece of incense, a sprig of herb or an essential oil possessing a scent with which you have no prior personal association, and which you feel is appropriate to the site. (For example, I might take frankincense to an Egyptian temple, or sage to a Native American holy site.) As you walk around the site, quietly smell the scent you have selected. Touch the place, too, where it is permissible to do so.

☆ Take lots of photographs of the monument, from all angles, as well as the surroundings – take a series of pictures to create a panorama of overlapping shots. If you have even a basic drawing ability, make a few sketches, for there is nothing like drawing a place or an object to make you see it.

☆ In addition to these activities, remember to spend some time just being at the place, allowing Lopez's 'fully dilated experience' to take place.

☆ As you leave, if it is permissible and non-harmful to do so, go into the vicinity of the site (not the site itself) and take a blade of grass, a leaf, a pebble or a small handful of soil or sand (but take nothing if it would cause noticeable material damage to the site or its surroundings, and *never* take any archaeological material from an ancient place).

☆ Later, collect together the photographs you took of the site, the associated scent of the place, and a tactile reminder (should you have been able to bring one back) and put them in a box. On one or two nights every week, go through this material, looking, touching, smelling and remembering, immediately before going to sleep. If a scent is involved, see that it is sprinkled on your bedclothes or in the air of the bedroom. Repeat this (it may take several weeks) until you have a dream about the place.

☆ However brief and inconsequential the dream might seem, make a written note of it and add that to your box of memorabilia.

☆ Keep doing this until your dreams about the place become more frequent and, perhaps, more complex. Note the imagery and associations that creep into your site dreams.

☆ Continue with this until you get to a point where no fresh dreams about the place seem to be occurring. Hopefully, by means of this process, which may take some months, you will develop a truly mythic relationship with the site you visited and will recover a little of the interaction that went on unconsciously between you and the site: the stream of information that slipped past your conscious mind.

6

Psychic Archaeology

Every visitor to an ancient sacred monument wishes they had a time machine that would allow them to see what happened at the place when it was first in use. During the course of the 20th century, various people have attempted to achieve this using what they believed to be psychic means.

The Gate of Remembrance

The first major instance of this kind on record was conducted by Frederick Bligh Bond during his investigations of Glastonbury Abbey. Bond, a recognised scholar of ecclesiastical architecture, was appointed director of excavations at the ruined abbey site in 1908. He felt that archaeology was 'hidebound' in that it failed to use intuition and other inner faculties alongside its logical, deductive work. He felt less constrained, and encouraged the notion of what he referred to as 'the training of the imaginative faculty along scientific lines and its application to archaeological research'. So he sought the assistance of psychic mediums who had the ability to write down 'spirit messages', a process known as 'automatic writing'. Bond did most of his psychic investigations using the abilities of John Bartlett, who was given the pseudonym 'John Alleyne' in Bond's writings. Bond would rest his fingers on Bartlett's hand while the medium wrote down material in a 'stream of consciousness' fashion in answer to questions posed by Bond. In the course of many sittings between 1907 and 1912, Bond amassed information in the form of diagrams and plans, and writings in Low Latin, Middle English, and modern English purporting to come from long-dead monks and other personages supposedly associated with Glastonbury Abbey in its heyday. Architectural information regarding the abbey site was offered in this manner, and Bond was apparently able to confirm some of this material by his excavations.

In his book, *The Gate of Remembrance* (1918), Bond unwisely revealed the unconventional source of his excavational guidance, and this had dire consequences for him professionally. He was ultimately barred from the abbey grounds and much of his archaeological evidence was tampered with. For a time, Bond removed himself to the United States, but eventually returned to Britain where he continued his enquiries into automatic writing until 1934. Bond was not a spiritualist, and rather than believing that the automatic writing was coming from dead souls, he preferred the hypothesis that some form of 'greater memory' belonging to the human race as a whole was involved, a concept in keeping with C.G. Jung's theory of a collective unconscious, and also with the occult idea of the 'Akashic Records', a kind of astral plane library.

Tuning in to the Past

Between the two world wars, it became fashionable among some investigators to bring along psychic mediums to ancient sites to see what they could 'pick up' — a form of psychic ability known as 'psychometry'. One woman noted for this gift was Geraldine Cummins, who was invited to work at two Irish sites by the archaeoastronomer, Admiral Boyle-Somerville. At one, the Three Fingers stones, she claimed to be able to see with her psychic vision elders who were able to 'draw power' from the stones and enter trance as a consequence. At the stone circle of Drumbeg, Cummins claimed to contact an entity which informed her that during a powerful midwinter ceremony held there 'Earth power' was drawn from the ground and used for a low, elemental form of magic. Prior to that, the entity said there had been a pure form of solar worship at the site.

The Scottish antiquarian and occultist, John Foster Forbes, brought another psychic, Iris Campbell, to the stone circle and outlier known as Long Meg and Her Daughters in Cumbria. The woman formed the psychic impression that the sites had operated as a 'receiving station' for 'Earth vibrations' from other sites, and could be used for the transmission of messages by pressing one's palms against them. The psychometrist also claimed that another site, Mayburgh Henge, also in Cumbria, was 'an experimental area . . . where magnetism was induced from the four points of the compass'. She said the place had been used to enhance the etheric centres in human beings.

Castlerigg, a stone circle in the same county, was visited by Geoffrey Hodson in 1922. Hodson was a renowned psychic, famous for his claimed ability to be able to see nature spirits or 'divas'. Hodson scanned the stone circle with his inner vision and psychically perceived a tall man with long dark hair and a beard, dressed in a flowing white garment, standing within the ring of stones, accompanied by other, similarly attired priests. They were engaged in a ritual in which energy visible to Hodson as a column of rosy-tinged opalescence was brought down from the sky and fused with the earth inside the stone circle. Hodson's mental snapshot included glimpses of banners depicting symbols draped over some of the stones.

America's 'sleeping prophet', Edgar Cayce, had found from a young age that when in a trance-like sleep he could respond to questions put to him on a wide range of subjects. He claimed that he was drawing his information from the Akashic Records, and gave over 14,000 such 'readings' amounting to nearly 50,000 pages of transcript during his lifetime. Cayce was best known for his readings on medical and nutritional matters, but he also 'read' the supposed past lives of clients, and, in particular, built up a vivid and detailed picture of Atlantis, and other lost civilisations. He claimed that evidence of Atlantean contact with ancient Egypt would be found in a Hall of Records hidden beneath the Sphinx, and to this day there are those who are actively trying to get this supposed secret chamber uncovered. As well as exotic readings like these, though, Cayce made more sober claims, for example that the Vikings had contacted the Americas and travelled inland. While this notion was out of the question in serious circles in Cayce's day, it is now widely accepted that Norsemen did visit the Americas before Columbus. He also claimed that the Sahara had once flowed with rivers, but it was only many years after Cayce's death in 1945 that long-dry river beds were mapped in the desert by space satellites.

In the 1970s, American explorer David Zink used the

impressions of psychics to enhance his visits to various ancient sites around the world. In his book, *The Ancient Stones Speak* (1979), Zink records that one of his psychic informants believed that the Scottish stone circle complex of Callanish was linked to the Pleiades in some mysterious way, creating disorienting energy vortices at the stones. Another claimed that the megalithic site of Hagar Qim on Malta had helped humans communicate with extraterrestrial beings. The Great Pyramid yielded many psychic impressions: that it was 'an energy collector and beacon', that its stones could precipitate out-of-body experiences, and of course, that it had been built by survivors of Atlantis. Zink noted that Geoffrey Hodson psychometrically saw rituals taking place on the Pyramid of the Sun in the ancient city of Teotihuacan, Mexico. Hodson interpreted the priests he perceived as being descendants of Atlanteans who were manipulating 'cosmic energies'. At Tiahuanaco, an ancient and mysterious city high in the Bolivian Andes near Lake Titicaca, a psychic told Zink that the famed Gate of the Sun present there had been moved to this location from elsewhere, a fact later confirmed archaeologically. However, she also said there was no cultivation in the area, but in recent years cultivation beds have been found, so this was wrong. Another psychic believed that the founders of the place came from Mars.

In the 1980s, the Dragon Project conducted experiments with psychometrists, in which psychics unknown to one another were taken to the Rollright Stones separately, and asked for their impressions. Little of what they said tallied with one another, but an example of information that did match was that two psychics independently claimed that a tribe from Scotland or the north had stayed for some time in the Rollright area.

If psychic information is to be used at a site, it is essential to separate fact from fantasy. There is no doubt, for instance, that Edgar Cayce's flights of fancy — for such they surely were — about lost civilisations has prevented scholars from taking any part of his readings seriously. This might be unfortunate, because in my own experiments with psychics, I have found that while most of their patter is rather dubious, an occasional fragment of hard information will stand out. You don't necessarily have to go along with a psychic's belief system or working mental model to accept that there may be extra-sensory ways of picking up fragments of authentic information. There is also no doubt that some people who fancy that they are picking up impressions at a site are simply deluding themselves, and by telling their fantasies they are deluding others. Be on your guard.

Remote Viewing

The 1970s saw the introduction of a more rigorous use of psychic archaeology, this time in the form of remote viewing — what used to be called clairvoyance. The American archaeological investigative team known as the Mobius Group made use of experts in remote viewing to help them identify the most fruitful spots at which to carry out archaeological excavations in and around Alexandria, in Egypt. Mobius would use odd-numbered groups of remote viewers — usually seven people — so as to establish majority consensus impressions. The psychics would be given an accurate but simplified map of the general target area, printed in a blue-green tone; this was because parapsychological experiments had indicated that too much detail and certain colours could hinder a remote viewer's sensing capabilities. Mobius further learned to put very precise questions to their panels of psychic advisers so as to avoid imprecise responses. They also had carefully controlled protocols in the handling of information between the team and the panel of psychics.

The Mobius Group notched up several positive results using this method. Their psychics predicted the remains of stone columns at a specific point in the harbour at Alexandria, where parts of a small palace at Timonium had formerly existed before coastal erosion. Mobius divers duly found broken remnants of three-foot-diameter columns of red Aswan granite. On another study, the group was seeking a long-lost palace on the tip of a peninsular that had been part of the ancient city of Alexandria. The area was now under water. Two remote viewers independently selected a very small area of the sea bed. A dive revealed an area on the sea floor marked by four huge granite blocks forming a platform. A substantial archaeological feature was definitely there that only future underwater excavation would be able to reveal in its entirety. Several similar successes followed.

In his book, *Psychic Archaeology* (1977), American researcher Jeffrey Goodman describes two powerful dreams in which he saw a place, apparently in south-west USA, where he uncovered archaeological evidence of previously unsuspected early human presence on the continent. These dreams led him to contact a remote viewer called Aron Abrahamsen. This man also claimed to be able to obtain additional information by accessing a universal psychic record, like Edgar Cayce, and receive messages from discarnate spirits. Goodman eventually located the spot he had seen in his dreams near Flagstaff, Arizona. Using psychic information from Abrahamsen, Goodman obtained evidence which he felt proved that the existence of Native Americans on the continent went back further than the normally accepted chronology.

Conducting Your Own Psychic Archaeology

You can try using psychometry yourself at ancient sites – it is really a form of primary sensing, a specialised extension of 'monumenteering'. Proceed with caution, however, and do not expect too much from your experiments if you are going to do them in a merely exploratory, casual way.

EXERCISE: PSYCHIC ARCHAEOLOGY

☆ When you are at a site, find a quiet spot. Stand or sit there, and close your eyes.

☆ Breathe slowly and evenly, and try to empty your mind of everything except the idea of the monument's past. If possible, rest your hands lightly on some old part of a monument.

☆ Register any impressions you get. Do not elaborate on them, or 'force' them – just keep yourself in 'reception mode'. Think of the impressions as birds flying freely into your mind, and try to catch them on the wing, so to speak.

☆ Be very careful not to construct complex fantasies; simply let the place speak to you. It is essential to believe wholeheartedly in the process of psychometry – at least while you are conducting your experiment. Ignore any doubts or cynicism – much of that is cultural baggage, and will in any case hamper your efforts.

☆ There are a couple of possible forms this basic procedure can take. If you have identified a magnetic stone at the site, then stand or sit next to it, laying your head lightly on it. The different magnetic field may help to stimulate the psychometric effort. Who knows if that was why it was put there originally? (Perhaps that is what Geraldine Cummins was referring to at the Three Fingers site.) It is helpful to believe that to be so, anyway, for the purposes of this experiment.

☆ You could also take a short nap rather than make a focused meditation. This happened spontaneously to me once at the Celtic holy well of Madron, in Cornwall. It was a warm afternoon, and I just laid myself out on a ledge in the tiny ruined chapel, where the healing waters welled up. I dozed off for about ten minutes, listening to the trickling water. I had an extremely vivid dream in which a pair of hands floated in front of my eyes, dipped into a pool of water, then massaged my eyes in a particular way. I awoke at once, still with a virtually tactile sense of the dream fingers working the muscles around my eyes. I immediately went over to the water and carried out the massage procedure I had just experienced in my dream. I was convinced that I had somehow tapped into how the healing waters had traditionally been applied long ago.

There is no way of assessing the objective truth of such impressions, of course. If you are simply performing psychic archaeology casually, out of curiosity, then that is fine, but if you want to develop it as a serious methodology in your Earth Mysteries work, you will need to get tougher with yourself. That means training, and for this you will need to enlist a helper. This person should supply you with small objects, one at a time, and then leave you to psychometrise each one. Write down whatever impressions you receive, if any. Later, check with your helper as to what the objects were, and their history. The objects might be someone's watch, or a piece from a museum or someone's personal collection. It doesn't matter what the object is, as long as it is something that you can check, and thereby assess the accuracy of any impressions received. Be aware that your impressions may not be straightforward visions, but could be just feelings, or fleeting images that relate to the object in round-about ways – they could be allegorical, metaphorical, or associative, like dreams. Before taking your site impressions too seriously, ensure that you are achieving at least moderate success with your psychometry exercises. If not, do not get into a deluding web of imagination, just cut your losses and realise that this approach is not for you. Always be honest with yourself when conducting subjective or experiential work. If you start deluding yourself, you will end up deluding others, and there is already far too much of that going on in the Earth Mysteries arena.

7

Shamanic Landscapes

There are certain types of monument that have up to now defied understanding – prehistoric ground markings forming, variously, linear and geometric images, or representational forms of animals and humanoid figures on a huge scale. These types of ritual landscape occur mainly in the Americas, though what may be similar features also occur in Europe and other parts of the Old World. It has only recently been realised that these strange ground markings are in effect the monuments of ancient shamanism, so I have termed them 'shamanic landscapes'.

Identifying Shamanic Landscapes

They are comprised of three basic identifiable characteristics:

☆ terrestrial effigies or 'geoglyphs'

☆ geometric and abstract meandering linear patterns

☆ straight line markings and 'roads'.

Locations such as the Nazca lines in Peru contain examples of all three categories together, but they can also occur in isolation. Any of these types of features can be constructed in any of the following ways, depending on terrain and local conditions:

☆ 'Petroforms' – outlines formed using small rocks and boulders laid on or pressed into the ground

☆ 'Intaglios' (an Italian word for a type of engraving) – markings scoured into desert surfaces

☆ Earthworks – usually low mounds shaped into human, animal, or geometric forms

☆ Engineered structures – in complex prehistoric Native American cultures the straight line markings seen at places like Nazca sometimes developed into more formalised constructions like royal roads and ceremonial causeways, as was the case with the ancient Maya.

Mystery Markings in the Americas

Shamanic landscapes are to be found scattered throughout the Americas, as even a brief and incomplete survey can indicate. Starting in the north, important sites occur in Whiteshell Provincial Park in Manitoba, Canada. In the last Ice Age glaciers here scraped bare expanses of granite bedrock which formed the surfaces on which petroform designs were laid out. The region was known as 'Manito Ahbee' to the Indians, meaning 'the place where God sits'.

Many of the petroforms are abstract or geometric, but some are figurative; there are even giant, petroform animal tracks! They are prehistoric in origin, but who made them and why is unknown, although present-day Indians in the region have a variety of beliefs about them. Saskatchewan, Alberta and British Columbia also boast examples of animal and human petroforms, and south of the Canadian border prehistoric petroform and earthen figures occur in various states.

The products of what archaeologists call the 'Effigy Mound Culture' are to be found in an area of northern midwest USA. Between AD 300 and 1300, perhaps as many as 10,000 earthen effigies were built, and even the fraction of these that survive are awe-inspiring and mysterious. Usually rising three or four feet above the surrounding ground level, these terrestrial sculptures have not yielded any burials (remains and/or attendant grave goods) or objects. While many are conical or cigar shaped, a good number are in the form of animals, humans or strange beings. The greatest concentration of surviving earthen effigies is to be found at Effigy Mounds National Monument in Iowa. This covers 1,475 acres and contains some 200 mounds. There are 26 animal figures, the largest being Great Bear Mound, which is 70 feet across at the shoulders and 130 feet in length. Another dramatic feature of the Iowa complex is a cluster of 13 effigies of birds and marching bears. All the animal effigies are accompanied by mounds displaying geometric and abstract shapes. The earthwork effigies of the northern United States also depict hybrid human-bird figures.

Perhaps the most famous earthern effigy is Serpent Mound in Adams County, Ohio. This stretches for about a quarter of a mile, and was probably built by the Adena people approximately 2,000 years ago. The serpentine mound stands four or five feet in height, and does not contain burials. The people

Serpent Mound, Ohio

who followed on from the Adena are known to archaeologists as the Hopewell culture. These Indians built complex and sophisticated geometric earthworks: precise circles, squares, parallelograms and hexagonal enclosures, some of them covering many acres, linked by linear causeways and avenues. In 1995, careful archaeological research, aided by infra-red air photography, revealed the course of a Hopewell road running dead straight for 60 miles through the Ohio countryside.

The south-western United States has a rich crop of shamanic landscapes of various kinds. A key example is the complex of 'roads' around Chaco Canyon in New Mexico, a cult centre of the lost Anasazi people. These 1,000-year-old Chacoan roads stretch for tens of miles around the canyon, linking now-ruined ceremonial 'Great Houses'. Where the roads meet the canyon rim, stairways were carved out of the rock walls reaching down to the canyon floor. These 30-foot-wide roads are not mere tracks, but engineered features. They are strikingly straight, and NASA infra-red surveys have revealed multiple parallel sections to some lengths of the roads. This has only deepened the mystery of the roads, as the Anasazi had neither wheeled vehicles nor horses. As Hosteen Beyal, a Navajo elder, told archaeologists in the 1920s: 'They may look like roads, but they are not roads.'

Other curious straight tracks were made by ancient Miwok Indians in the California sierras. Over this rugged terrain they ran 'with airline directness' as described by one archaeologist. In the extreme south of California, prehistoric American Indians used desert etchings, lines of boulders, and earthworks to mark out strange geometric patterns, enclosures and meanders. Ancient patterns can be found on the shimmering-hot floor of Death Valley, or the Chocolate Mountains in Imperial County, near the California–Mexico border. The figures are etched into the desert surface, or outlined with small rocks. Serpentine lines of stones can meander for hundreds of metres, connecting with cellular-like enclosures. Although these look like casual images, they have been found to contain fixed 'sighting stones' of unusual colour or shape, suggesting that they were planned constructions. In California's Mojave Desert numerous examples of ground figures are to be found, notably the giant effigies 15 miles north of Blythe. These desert intaglios include three large human figures, big cats, a concentric circle and a spiral. The tallest figure measures about 170 feet. Other ground figures along the Colorado River terraces include further human-shaped figures, and giant depictions of rattlesnakes, lizards, and mountain lions. Some of the ground markings are thought to date back as much as 3,000 years.

In Mexico, there are several shamanic landscapes, a notable example being that around the prehistoric citadel of La Quemada in Zacatecas. About 100 miles of ancient roads have been discovered in this area, dating to between AD 700 and 800. They are masonry structures. These 'perfectly straight' roads, as an early archaeologist described them, not only linked buildings and plazas at the La Quemada site, but also extended to cliff faces, to caves and to apparently nowhere in particular. Some of these strange roads had altars on them.

Mexico's Yucatan peninsula was the heartland of the ancient Maya, whose culture flowered between the late 3rd century AD and 900 AD. They built long, straight roads which today's Maya call *sacbeob* ('white ways'). These interconnected plazas and temples within some of the Mayan ceremonial cities, and also linked cities themselves. They now exist only in fragmentary sections, the longest-known surviving *sacbe* (singular) being the 62-mile-long section that runs between Coba and Yaxuna in the northern part of the peninsula. This was discovered by explorer Thomas Gann in the 1920s. He described it as 'a great elevated road ... 32-feet wide ... built of great blocks of cut stone ... straight as an arrow, and almost flat as a rule'. Altars, arches and curious ramps are associated with the *sacbeob*, and according to local Mayan tradition the physical network of the *sacbeob* is augmented at various places by non-material underground *sacbeob* and others that run through the air known as *Kusam Sum*. The vast Mayan territory extended south through modern-day Belize, Guatemala, El Salvador and Honduras, and *sacbe* segments are known of throughout much of this region.

NASA have also employed sophisticated electronic aerial photography techniques to image paths running through the mountainous rainforest of the Arenal area of Costa Rica. These paths, which 'follow relatively straight lines' despite the difficult terrain, have been examined at ground level and dated to a period between AD 500 and 1200. Researchers have discovered that the paths are 'death roads': one goes straight over the top of a hill, rather than round it, linking a village with an ancient cemetery.

In South America, the Nazca lines in Peru are the best-known example of these kind of landscape features. They were first discovered in 1926 by Peruvian archaeologists. Twenty years later, Paul Kosok of Long Island University saw the lines as 'the largest astronomy book in the world'. He passed this conviction on to Maria Reiche, a German mathematician, who walked, mapped, and lived with the lines for half a century until her death in 1998. She was disappointed with Gerald Hawkins of the Smithsonian Institution, who in 1968 carried out ground, aerial and computer surveys of the desert lines. Hawkins was already famous for 'decoding' Stonehenge as a prehistoric astronomical computer, but his studies at Nazca showed no significant astronomical orientations.

The best work on the Nazca markings took place over several seasons in the 1980s by a team of investigators co-ordinated by astronomer Anthony Aveni of Colgate University, New York. The team compiled extensive new information on the features. Maria Reiche had noted what she called 'star-like centres', which were raised hillocks or promontories that lines seemed to radiate from or converge on to. These centres were also connected one to another by lines. The new investigators confirmed this finding, and uncovered many more such 'line centres', as they came to be called. It was also found that numerous lines contained deeply worn footpaths, suggesting that they had been used for repetitive walking or pilgrimages, though it was not clear what the purpose of such activity had been. Detailed mapping of the lines indicated that at least some seemed associated with old cemeteries out on the pampa, and also with ancient aqueducts and arroyos (the dried beds of occasional streams).

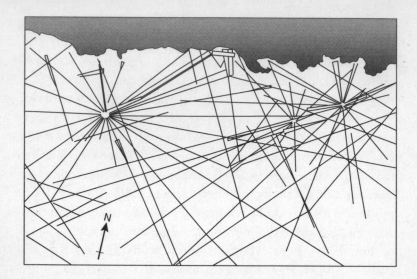

Plan of the Nazca pampa and the network of lines

Broken pottery – probably left as votive offerings – was found at associated sites.

The popular association with the Nazca lines tends to be Erich von Däniken's assertion that they were landing strips for ancient astronauts – a kind of prehistoric space centre. But the pampa surface is so delicate that footprints left by Kosok over half a century ago are still evident. The markings made by landing spacecraft on the Nazca 'runways', and the blast effects of their rockets, jets or other propulsion systems would still be clearly visible; they aren't. Von Däniken then tried to assert that perhaps the lines were *themselves* the tracks of spacecraft, but it can be shown that they were, in fact, constructed features. And as the late Carl Sagan remarked, why would a spaceship capable of crossing light years of space need a landing strip like one of our relatively primitive aircraft? In his book, *Chariots of the Gods?*, von Däniken showed a photograph of rounded markings on the Nazca

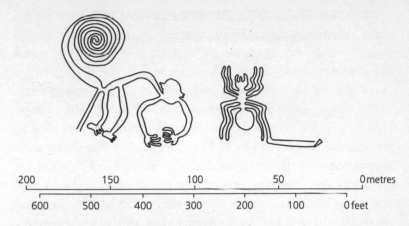

200   150   100   50   0 metres

600   500   400   300   200   100   0 feet

Two of the ground figures found at Nazca

pampa, remarking that they were reminiscent of aircraft parking bays at airports. In fact, the photo showed part of the leg of a giant bird etched on the desert. Above all, as you can learn for yourself in this chapter, the exceptional straightness of the lines is a characteristic of linear ground markings and 'roads' found throughout ancient America.

The markings on the pampa near Nazca, and at several other locations in the Andes, consist not only of straight lines but include all the characteristics of 'shamanic landscapes' – beautifully symmetrical ground drawings of animals, insects, flowers, reptiles, birds, geometrical forms like spirals and parallelograms, as well as weird abstract shapes.

Hundreds of miles to the south-east are even more remarkable 'lines' that criss-cross the high plain of western Bolivia. Some of these lines are 20 miles long, considerably longer than any found at Nazca. French anthropologist Alfred Métraux came across them in the 1930s, when he investigated shrines set out in a straight row from a small village and found them to be standing on a pathway that was 'absolutely straight, regardless of the irregularities of the ground'. In more recent years, British explorer Tony Morrison conducted an expedition to study the lines, noting that they crossed ridges and valleys without deviation. The lines are, in the main, simply ways cut through the bush and cleared of any debris. The shrines along them are of various kinds – Christianised adobe structures, piles of rocks, places where lightning has struck, and similar sanctified spots. There were also churches standing on some of the lines, as at the community of Sajama, for instance. The Quechua word the Indians applied to the lines or paths was *siq'i*, meaning 'a row of things'. What the lines had originally been for, the Indians either did not themselves remember or were not telling Morrison.

Prehistoric straight roads also occur in the lowland, rain-forest areas of South America, east of the Andes. Over 900 miles of causeways have been reported and studied to a limited extent in the upper Amazon region of north-eastern Bolivia. One investigator, William Denevan, remarks that the features are 'unusually straight'. At least some of them seem to connect burial and ceremonial sites, and he makes the important point that while engineering a straight road in flat terrain is not all that difficult, 'building a long straight road to a destination that cannot be seen is not easy'. Further, he notes that the causeways occur in dry, drained ground and not just in wetlands, and thus they take on 'other significance' than can be explained merely by providing dry transport across swamp country. Elsewhere, knowledge of prehistoric roads is still extremely sketchy.

The Meaning of the Markings

Because these landscape features were made long before Columbus reached the Americas, we have no documentation to tell us what they were all about. We can only make deductions and interpretations from the evidence that exists. The first realisation that Earth Mysteries researchers and a few brave anthropologists came to was that as far as could be determined, these complexes of ground markings occurred in the territories of people who had been – and in a few cases still are – shamanistic.

A few examples will illustrate this. The Hopewell people, who built the earthen effigies, straight ceremonial roads and geometric earthworks in Ohio, are known to have been a coalition of tribes who all shared the same shamanistic religion. The burial mounds of Hopewell shamans have been excavated and certain features found: bird claws cut out of mica that were hung on shaman's robes symbolising the spirit flight of the shaman in trance; wooden effigies of hallucinogenic mushrooms; and antler headgear – antlers were worn by shamans in many parts of the world, especially in Siberia, the home of classical shamanism. The Pueblo Indians of the American Southwest were all shamanic, their shamans using mixtures of the mind-altering Jimson Weed (one of the favoured hallucinogens of Carlos Castanada's supposed mentor, Don Juan). The La Quemada complex is acknowledged by the Huichol Indians who still maintain a shamanism based on the hallucinogenic peyote cactus, and every spring equinox they hold a peyote ceremony there; the rest of the year they purposefully ignore the place. The ancient Maya arose out of rainforest shamanic tribes and, ultimately, collapsed back into them. These people are still there, using a variety of plant hallucinogens as the basis of their shamanism. In South America, Amazon tribes still practise a hallucinogen-based shamanism, often using ayahuasca, a mind-altering drug mixture based on Banisteriopsis, the 'soul vine'.

And the Nazca lines? Well, nearly 1,000 years before the

Nazca culture, a great shamanic religion developed in northern Peru known to archaeologists as the Chavin culture. The centre of this religion was a remarkable temple known as Chavin de Huantar which has wall carvings showing hallucinogens such as the San Pedro cactus, and sequences of faces distorting as if in hallucinogenic visions. The influence of the Chavin culture extended for hundreds of miles through the Andes and lasted for hundreds of years. The societies that succeeded it were also shamanistic. It was out of this background that the makers of the Nazca lines emerged.

So, the mystery markings were the products of shamanistic peoples. The markings themselves, because they were all so different, appear to have had varying meanings. The animal and human ground figures may in some cases have represented mythic personalities and served general tribal ceremonial purposes, but many probably depicted spirits and shamanic 'familiars' or power animals. The hybrid human-bird figures almost certainly related to the out-of-body sense of spirit flight produced by the native hallucinogens taken by the shamans to promote trance states. Taken together, these ground figures were probably intended to ward off the flying spirits of enemy sorcerers and shamans from neighbouring tribes.

Alongside some of the meandering patterns and complex enclosures are circular stone settings, thought to have been used by shamans as 'rings of power' for their seances or vision quests. There are also features identified as shamans' hearths. These obviously demonstrate the shamanic nature of these curious ground figures, while some markings may have been dance grounds for ceremonial or ritual purposes. Anthropological evidence indicates that at least some of the meandering lines in the American Southwest were part of a magical geography and represented symbolic 'mountain ranges' laid out by tribal shamans to block the influence of hostile shamans.

The straight-line features are difficult to interpret. The engineered, causeway-type straight ways have been considered as military and trade routes by some cautious scholars, but this view is increasingly finding less favour with informed archaeological investigators. Although everyone agrees that some of these features served several simultaneous roles in ancient American societies, it is their ceremonial and ritual aspects that require the greatest attention. The simpler desert lines, like those at Nazca, were clearly religious in some way, rather than trade routes or military roads. One leading investigator, the late John Hyslop, stated that prehistoric Native American roads had meanings and uses not found in our present-day idea of roads, and he warned that attempts to interpret all aspects of them in purely materialistic terms are bound to fail.

If the lines and roads were shamanic, or derived from earlier shamanic beliefs, as seems certain, why the obsession with straightness? This is their fundamental characteristic, found throughout the Americas. It is unlikely that their specific cultural meanings were all the same, but their essential *form* clearly is. It suggests some universal factor, common to all peoples. American anthropologist, Marlene Dobkin de Rios, suggested in 1977 that the lines, however they were later developed, derived their basic linearity from a mental phenomenon called 'entoptic patterns' experienced in shamanic trance. These are recognisable sets of geometric 'form constants' that are produced in the human brain during certain stages of trance, and seen as vivid, dancing, repetitive patterns by the person undergoing the trance. Because they belong to the neuronal 'wiring' of all human beings they occur in all societies and in all periods in which trance states

Prehistoric rock art patterns like these at Newgrange, Ireland, are now thought to be based on mental imagery generated in trance states.

have been induced. Although different meanings may have been placed on these patterns by different societies in different places and times, the actual forms themselves remain recognisable. Some Amazon Indian tribes are known to use these patterns as the basis for their decorative art, and give the specific patterns or form constants their own meanings. Quite recently, some archaeologists have shown that entoptic imagery can be detected in prehistoric rock art at various sites around the world, including the Americas.

Even in our modern culture, we are fairly familiar with one classic entoptic form constant, namely the 'tunnel' image often reported in the accounts of those who undergo near-death and out-of-body experiences. A very important property of this particular entoptic image is that it often heralds the moment when the person stops merely observing the geometric and patterned motifs, and begins to feel as if he or she is floating down the tunnel into the otherworldly realm, often seen at first as a bright light.

Dobkin de Rios claimed the landscape lines were effectively depictions of this type of entoptic motif, and the fact that they seemed to have been designed to be seen from above was because they related to the aerial journey or out-of-body spirit flight of the shaman. (This dispenses with modern notions of 'ancient astronauts'.) We do not necessarily have to believe that this literally happened, but if the makers of the lines did so, then that is all that matters. To this day, village shamans in Mexico take Jimson Weed in order to fly, so they believe, to visit other villages at night. American anthropologist Weston le Barre has emphasised this sense of soul flight that many native plant hallucinogens specifically promote.

The linear ground-markings might have represented spirit trajectories or routes. (It is worth noting that in Bushman rock art in southern Africa, the out-of-body trance produced during their 'trance dances' is depicted by a line.) In this view, the desert lines were a form of spirit geography. However, it is likely that this would only have been the original association with the lines, a secret belonging to the shamans and priests, and it would have been presented in outward, religiously dogmatic ways to ordinary tribal members, eventually taking on ceremonial and royal connotations as societies grew larger and more complex.

Otherworld Roads

The idea that straight ground markings and mystery 'roads' may have represented routes believed to have been taken by entranced shamans in the otherworld (which was always seen as located within the physical fabric of the material environment) is not mere supposition. In 1990, Alan Ereira filmed the remote Kogi Indians of northern Colombia for the BBC. The Kogi have preserved deep pre-Columbian traits and are ruled by a shamanic elite. These shamans explained to Ereira that their roads held spiritual significance for them, and that the Earth Mother had instructed them that the roads must be constantly walked – a similar idea to this would explain the deep ruts formed by ancient feet inside some of the Nazca lines. Further, they showed him a stone road that was straight and which they said was the trace of a spirit path they took when in the spirit otherworld. They pointed out that such spirit routes could be 'seen' by them even where they were not marked by physical roads. The Kogi also have a standing stone criss-crossed with straight lines, and this is a map of the spirit paths in the Kogi territory; only some of these had physical 'traces'. You can see some of these findings in Ereira's BBC video, *From the Heart of the World*.

This method of interpreting the mystery of linear ground markings has been dubbed the 'spirit line' approach. Not only does it open up a whole new direction of Earth Mysteries research, it has had a profound effect on the issue of leys or ley lines, causing some controversy and confusion both inside and outside Earth Mysteries circles. In the next chapter, we will try to clarify this muddle.

8

The Ley Story

The idea of leys is a significant Earth Mysteries theme. You probably have a vague notion that leys are energy lines of some kind that can cause personal problems for inhabitants of buildings standing on them. In fact, the whole ley business is a conceptual jungle, and is consequently the most misunderstood and misreported topic in the whole field of Earth Mysteries. This is particularly unfortunate from the point of view of those who want to engage in 'hands on' activities, because 'ley hunting' has traditionally been one of the most practical of Earth Mysteries pursuits. It is important, then, to untangle this messy business. The starting point has to be the background of the whole matter, for there is little point in discussing any subject if we do not know when and why it originated, or how it subsequently developed.

The Origins of the Ley Idea

The classic definition of a ley is that it is an alignment, a straight line, of ancient sites. The greater the number of sites

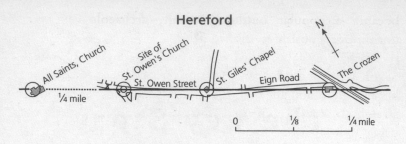

Hereford

One of Watkins's Herefordshire leys

or other 'ley marker points' there are along a ley, the more accurately it can be marked on a map. The idea of such ancient alignments achieved its fullest expression in the work of English businessman, pioneer photographer, inventor and amateur archaeologist, Alfred Watkins. In 1921, while looking at a map of his home area of Herefordshire and Welsh border countryside, he suddenly noticed that various prehistoric places, such as standing stones, earthen burial mounds, prehistoric earthworked hills, and other similar features appeared to fall into alignments. Watkins reached for a long ruler and confirmed this intuition, finding that he could indeed draw straight lines through three, four, and sometimes five or more ancient places marked on a single sheet of a one-inch-to-the-mile Ordnance Survey map. He went on to spend several years studying such alignments on the ground and on maps. He used his pioneering photography skills to take photographs of features and views of his alignments, and wrote books and gave lectures on the subject. His most important book on leys, *The Old Straight Track*, was first published in 1925. In response to his work, the Straight Track Club was formed, in which members around the country undertook field research and exchanged postal portfolios on their findings, and would periodically gather for picnics at interesting ley marker points. Although ley hunting became a popular outdoor pursuit, archaeologists were unanimously hostile to the whole idea.

Watkins initially called his alignments 'leys', an Anglo-Saxon word meaning meadows or cleared strips of ground, because he thought that the lines were the remnants of straight traders' tracks laid down by Stone Age surveyors using sighting rods, a line-of-sight ranging method that he claimed led to the straightness of the old tracks. Watkins's vision was of straight tracks running from one hilltop to another 'like a fairy chain', and where they cut through forested valleys, strips of ground were cleared, hence, 'ley'. However, he never seemed at ease with this term, and by 1929 he referred to his alignments only as 'old straight tracks', 'archaic tracks', and occasionally 'sighted tracks', meaning pathways or roads aligned to landmarks such as earthworked hills.

There had been others who had made similar claims about ancient alignments in Britain, America, France and Germany from at least the 18th century. In the United States, for example, Indian trader Walter Pidgeon claimed in his book, *Traditions of Dee-Coo-Dah*, 1858, that the pre-Columbian Indian mounds in the Midwest were laid out in 'lineal ranges'. Like some early British alignment researchers, the 'German School' tended to associate aligned sites with ancient astronomy, but Watkins's German contemporary, Wilhelm Teudt, was talking about virtually the same idea as leys with his *heilige Linien* ('holy lines'). Unfortunately, much of the German linear research became associated with Nazi philosophy, and was suppressed after World War Two.

Watkins noted that he often found ancient churches falling on his leys. He assumed this was because the old straight tracks eventually fell into disuse, leaving only aligned sites to indicate their former course, and that in the early centuries of the Christian era some of these pagan sites became Christianised. There is no doubt that some prehistoric sites were Christianised, in that churches were built on earthworks, or megaliths were incorporated into the fabric of church buildings, but whether this happened on the scale that Watkins's theory required remains open to question.

Alfred Watkins died in 1935. The following year, the occultist Dion Fortune wrote a novel, *The Goat-Foot God*, in which she introduced the notion of 'lines of force' connecting megalithic sites. In 1938, Arthur Lawton, a member of the Straight Track Club, wrote a paper in which he claimed that leys were lines of cosmic force that could be dowsed. He was impressed with German dowsing claims that there were noxious rays and forces coming from some points in the ground, and with the work of French dowsers who were stating that prehistoric standing stones were placed over the crossings of underground streams. In 1948, the Straight Track Club closed down as there were only a few surviving members, and the idea of leys was kept alive by a few fringe writers and researchers.

The Ley Hunting Revival

Leys took on a new lease of life from 1960, due to an ex-RAF pilot, Tony Wedd. He was very interested in flying saucers or UFOs, and had read Watkins's *The Old Straight Track* and also a French book, *Flying Saucers and the Straight Line Mystery* (1958), by Aimé Michel, in which it was suggested that UFO sightings during a 1954 French flying saucer outbreak fell into straight lines or 'orthotenies'. (This was shown many years later to be a mistake.) Wedd decided that Watkins's leys and Michel's orthotenies were one and the same phenomenon. He had also read a book by the American Buck

Nelson called *My Trip to Mars, the Moon and Venus* (1956), in which it was claimed that flying saucers used energy from 'magnetic currents' flowing through the Earth. In addition, Wedd would also have read the best-selling *Flying Saucers Have Landed* (1953) by UFO contactee George Adamski and Desmond Leslie. In that book, Leslie also speculates about UFOs following 'magnetic paths' across the planet – perhaps where Nelson actually got the notion. In 1961, Wedd published a pamphlet in which he theorised that UFO occupants flew along magnetic lines of force linking ancient sites which acted as landmarks for UFO pilots. Though we might think that this sounds more like the ideas of an old-fashioned plane pilot than the activities of alien astronauts with interstellar technology, Wedd formed a group with a mission to make contact with the 'Space Brothers'. It enlisted the aid of a psychic who referred to 'lines of force' and 'magnetic nodes' in the landscape, and who channelled communications from supposed extra-terrestrial beings. Two members of this group, Jimmy Goddard and Philip Heselton, set up a ley hunters' club in 1962, and three years later founded *The Ley Hunter* journal. They managed a few issues of the modest publication.

Leys went on to find their niche in the new wave of enthusiasm for all matters occult – including UFOs and ancient mysteries – that swept through the psychedelic decade, and merged with the growth of Earth Mysteries interest, as described in Chapter 1. In 1969, John Michell published *The View Over Atlantis*, in which he brought his erudition and insight to bear on the ley theory, and mixed it with esoteric geometrical and number systems, feng shui, and dowsing. This book had a profound influence on the new generation of ley hunters. In that same year, *The Ley Hunter* journal started to be published again, under the editorship of Paul Screeton.

(Under the later editorship of myself, followed by architect Danny Sullivan, it remained in continuous publication until 1999.) In 1972, Janet and Colin Bord published their widely read and richly illustrated *Mysterious Britain*, in which they summarised the new wave of ideas about leys and combined them with themes from folklore. In 1974, Paul Screeton published *Quicksilver Heritage*, in which he further amplified ideas about leys, Earth energies and mystic, occult themes. In this same year, the first article on leys was published in the United States by the then president of the American Society of Dowsers, Terry Ross. He mentioned leys only as lines of energy. This was picked up and amplified by various elements in dowsing circles and the New Age movement in America, where there was little knowledge of Alfred Watkins, or the original old straight track theory. In 1976, British dowser Tom Graves published a new book on dowsing (*Dowsing: Techniques and Applications*, 1976) in which he reinforced the idea of dowsing energies along what were now becoming known as 'ley lines'.

Two Schools of Ley Hunting

By the end of the 1970s, ley hunters had begun to split into two camps, one considering leys as lines of energy, while the other was more research-oriented, studying actual alignments in the landscape. The idea of energy lines became the more popular, and from that time on was an unquestioned tenet of New Age belief. The camp engaged in more grounded research on the ley subject, on the other hand, had studied the 'energy line' idea and found it to be based on subjective notions. However, they also came to realise that Alfred Watkins's idea of leys as old straight tracks was also untenable, because the British Isles have been extensively photographed from the air since Watkins's time and air photographs can show where ground was disturbed even thousands of years ago. There is simply no evidence of any system of old straight tracks. Also, protracted debate with statisticians had made some of the research-based ley hunters more aware of the surprising role chance can play in the aligning of sites, especially with regard to lines drawn on maps involving sites of many different types and ages.

Investigators of the research-based school are now often referred to as 'the new ley hunters' which is ironic as they have been showing since 1988 that leys do not exist as separate features identifiable in their own right. Even more ironic is the fact that although they proclaim leys as a dead issue, the new ley hunters have become involved in the study of mystery landscape lines of various kinds, such as the actual, physical features forming the 'shamanic landscapes' of the Americas as described in Chapter 7, and also in unexplained linear features in Europe and other parts of the Old World, deriving from both archaeology and folklore.

Death Roads

The oldest type of mystery landscape line in Britain is the Neolithic cursus. Cursuses are earthen avenues formed by ditches and banks, with square or rounded ends where these survive. They link long barrows and other types of burial mound, and range from a few hundred metres to a mile or two in length. Some cursuses are perfectly straight, others are straight in sections, simply changing axis at certain points, while yet others have straight sections linked by curvilinear segments. The term 'cursus' is Latin for race-course, and this misnomer resulted from the discovery of the Stonehenge cursus by William Stukeley in 1723. He thought it was a Romano-British racecourse, and so gave it the Latin name. Although this kind of site is much older than Roman times, dating back over 4,000 years, and is a complete mystery, the name has stuck. About 50 have so far been discovered since Stukeley's time. They are mainly visible only as crop markings from the air, though remains of earthworks can still be seen at ground level on a few of them. Excavation has revealed little about the purpose or function of cursuses, but they typically occur in Neolithic ritual landscapes associated with henge monuments. The new ley hunters point out that cursuses link the idea of straightness with death, and therefore quite probably with spirits. They suggest that cursuses may have been spirit paths or enclosures associated with ceremonial activities by religious functionaries – perhaps Stone Age shamans.

Next in terms of age are Bronze Age stone rows found on Dartmoor in southern England, and elsewhere. They are associated with burial sites, usually extending from them in one or more directions. The suggestion is that they are spirit paths or routes of some kind because of this association, and because they often have what archaeologists call 'blocking stones' at their ends, looking literally as if they are blocking something. This is curiously reminiscent of the ancient Chinese landscape divination system of feng shui, which had devices for blocking spirits coming into a building, temple, or tomb.

Leaping ahead over 2,000 years to the medieval period, we find a number of linear features that were specifically regarded as death roads. In Sweden, for instance, a totally straight ritual road leading to a Viking cemetery has been excavated; this was used ceremonially to carry the body of the dead chieftain to his rest. In Holland, there are *Doodwegen*, 'death roads', which were also sometimes called *Spokenwegen*, 'spook roads', which converged on cemeteries. Some of these funerary paths survive in fragments to this day, and are notable for their straightness. Indeed, it was illegal to carry a corpse in anything other than a straight line to burial in medieval Holland. In Germany, there is a mysterious paved path known as the *Steinweg*, 'stone way', on the Wurmberg in the Harz Mountains, a region that was notorious as the gathering place of night-flying witches. It runs straight across the summit plateau of the mountain to a stone ring containing a burial kist – a kind of prehistoric stone box set into the ground containing the remains of the dead – dating to at least the Iron Age. Despite the prehistoric dates of the stone rings, however, pollen analysis shows that the *Steinweg*, strangely, dates to between the 11th and 13th centuries AD.

In Britain, death roads were known as corpse ways, coffin lines, and lychways, among various other names. These are mainly medieval paths or tracks leading to certain church cemeteries along which walking funerals were conducted from homes in outlying parts of the parish. Although British corpse ways do not share the dead straightness of their Continental counterparts, they very often followed generally direct routes.

Spirit Ways

The new ley hunters think death roads and corpse ways have considerable bearing on the notion of leys in two ways. First, it appears that Alfred Watkins may have inadvertently included medieval corpse ways in what he considered to be his ley alignments. The second reason is deeper: the corpse path tradition, while serving a pragmatic purpose in a fairly defined period of European history, possibly enshrined fragmentary, half-forgotten beliefs in spirit ways originating in earlier times. These perhaps ultimately reach back to very ancient European and Asian shamanism, just as with the shamanic landscapes in ancient America. For instance, it was considered 'unlucky' to take a corpse to burial by a route other than the customary corpse way. What this *really* meant was that if the body was not taken by this route, the spectre of the departed might wander the land as a lost soul. In Irish custom, this was further implied by an insistence that the feet of the corpse be always kept pointing away from the family home on its journey along the corpse way to the cemetery. As an additional measure to help prevent haunting, the corpse path usually passed through streams, crossroads, ancient stiles and various other 'betwixt and between' locations, all of which were thought to prevent or hinder the free passage of spirits. (The corpses of suicides were buried at crossroads, for instance, so that their spirits would be 'bound' there. For similar reasons, gallows were often erected at such spots. Interestingly, ancient crossroads were valid ley marker points according to Watkins.)

In olden times people feared spirits walking abroad, especially at night and certain times of the year, like All Hallows (Hallowe'en) and New Year's Eve. This is shown by widespread folk customs such as the sweeping of old paths and crossroads to clear them of spirits, and the erection of devices known as spirit traps, which essentially consisted of a net or tangle of threads, at the entrances of houses or on old, rarely used tracks – especially those leading from a cemetery. There were many variations of this kind of device.

A further confirmation is that in addition to physical death roads, there are other 'paths' of Old Europe and elsewhere that are invisible, though in the folk mind they had a definite geography. In Germany, there were the *Geisterwege*, 'spirit paths'. These were invisible but were located in specific places known to local folk who avoided them because they were thought to be where ghosts were likely to be encountered. The paths were said to run in straight lines over mountains and valleys and through marshes. In the towns they passed close to houses or went right through them. The paths ended or originated in a cemetery. In Ireland, there were the famous 'fairy passes': invisible paths that ran from one *rath* (prehistoric earthwork) to another. It is unclear as to whether these fairy routes were straight or not, but Irish lore implies that they were. It was considered unwise to build on the course of a fairy pass; to do so would be to invite bad luck.

This is curiously reminiscent of the Chinese system of landscape divination, feng shui, in which straight features in the landscape – roads, ridges, river courses and lines of trees – all facilitated the passage of troublesome spirits. If a tomb or building was on the course of such a 'secret arrow' in the land, then preventative measures had to be taken. This same belief is echoed in Indonesia, where some temples have low walls inside their main entrances to deflect any straight-moving spirits from getting inside the sacred precinct. In Laos, the Hmong have a rule that a new house in a village should not be built directly in front or directly behind another house. This is because they believe that spirits travel in straight lines, and when corpses are moved from the house for burial they must go on a straight course. A similar system existed in the Gilbert Islands, in the Pacific Ocean, where there was a ritual known as 'Straightening the Way of the Dead'.

In addition, spirit-and-line ideas were associated in folklore with threads and string. Australian Aborigine healers used a filament secreted by an insect to act as a 'road' for a sick person's spirit to return to their body, and Siberian

Buryat shamans used taut threads as spirit roads in both healing and in shamanic initiation. There are many other examples.

In the new ley hunting, then, old views about leys, whether Watkins's old straight tracks or New Age energy lines, are no longer considered valid. This is an unavoidable result of research knowledge acquired over a quarter of a century and more. There nevertheless remain linear features on ancient landscapes in both the Old and New Worlds that require explanation.

The Spirit Line Theory

It seems that to the ancient mind in various parts of the world, straight lines of all kinds – whether marks on the ground, folk concepts or threads – were associated with the passage of spirits. Curved, twisted or jumbled lines, on the other hand, were thought by our forebears to bind spirits. In trying to get to the heart of this belief system, the new 'spirit line' ley hunters have made the link with the shamanic landscapes of the Americas: the recurring straightness element surviving in many of the Old World features and beliefs is seen as originating in similar shamanic traditions, involving the aerial flight of the shaman's spirit and the entoptic patterns and motifs occurring in trance as seems to be the case with the Native American lines. It is known that shamanistic traits were carried over the Bering Straits by the migrating people from Siberia who became the American Indians, so was this spirit line concept part of that cultural baggage?

It has to be stressed that this spirit line approach is in its infancy, and some people interested in Earth Mysteries are resisting it. Those who are sceptical about Earth Mysteries in general are anxious to stamp on a theory such as this, which can claim scholarly evidence to support it and is therefore seen as especially dangerous to conservative academic opinion, while those who want to dowse energy lines do not want their beliefs and activities disturbed.

The spirit line theory is about ten years old in its present form, and it certainly needs much more work (only the briefest outline has been possible here). It is generally reckoned that a valid new theory in any field takes about 15 years to establish itself, so the idea of 'spirit lines' has about five years to go from the start of the new millennium before it begins to be generally absorbed. What can be said at the moment is that of all approaches to the ley issue, the spirit line theory makes best use of authentic anthropological and archaeological data and most closely relates to the way ancient people actually saw the world. You will have to weigh up your own opinions about it.

Practical Ley Hunting Today

If you find yourself tending towards a spirit line approach, old ideas of ley hunting activities such as drawing straight lines all over maps, or wandering around fields with dowsing rods trying to follow leys, will hold little interest. But there is still practical work that can be done. Here is a basic outline for a useful course of action for 'new ley hunting'.

☆ Obtain a copy of Alfred Watkins's *The Old Straight Track* or his slightly later *The Ley Hunter's Manual*. There have been modern editions of both books, but in case of difficulty your library will be able to obtain them for you. Although his ideas as a whole are now redundant, Watkins was an old countryman, and his books contain valuable insights into the landscape and provide a charming read.

☆ Learn how to read maps, and to use grid references. There are books that can help you to do this, including my own *The New Ley Hunter's Guide* (see Further Reading). Basic information is also usually given in AA road map books, and in the margins of Ordnance Survey maps.

☆ Visit some visible ancient mystery lines so you can sense the reality of what has been discussed. Why not try out some of your monumenteering techniques at them? In particular, note how these linear features relate to other points in the landscape, and feel the distinct sensation of standing on some of these ancient ways made perhaps for spirits rather than human beings . . .

In Britain, look for cursuses and stone rows – the Ordnance Survey 1:50,000 and 1:25,000 scale maps show a fair proportion of both types of monument. A good cursus to start with is the one half a mile north of Stonehenge. This is nearly two miles long and aligns on to the remains of a long barrow. A byway leads past the Stonehenge car park, and you walk along this until you reach a National Trust sign which announces that you are standing on the cursus. If you look hard, you will be able to make out the ridges forming its edges, but there are National Trust notice boards at points all along its length giving you a bird's eye view of the feature from that location. Another cursus worth visiting is the Dorset Cursus on Cranbourne Chase, near Blandford Forum. The south-western end is at map grid reference ST 969124 and the earthworks here are still quite substantial. You will be able to see the course of the cursus running up a hill slope towards a long barrow.

Again in Britain, Dartmoor is a good area in which to seek stone rows. Two I would recommend are the Merrivale rows just off the trans-Dartmoor B3357 road at map grid reference

SX 555747. Here you will see twin rows of small standing stones some hundreds of yards in length, with distinctive blocking stones at their ends. Another fascinating stone row complex is on Shovel Down in the north-east corner of the moor, west of Chagford at map grid reference SX 659861. Here stone rows radiate out from a burial site, and you will note that one of them aligns to the Scorhill stone circle about a mile to the north.

In the United States, a major centre of an ancient straight 'roads' system is Chaco Canyon in New Mexico, located south of Farmington. Apart from being a fascinating place, with Anasazi ruins littering the canyon floor, there is a good interpretation centre and you can get maps showing some of the mysterious Chacoan roads. The best vantage point is at Pueblo Alto, a ruin on the canyon's northern rim. Several roads converge here, and a notice board shows you their location. It is difficult but not impossible to detect the courses of some of the 1,000-year-old mystery features – you just need to train your eye. A tip: wait until a few minutes before sunset, and you will fleetingly see the course of the roads showing up as soft shadowy lines.

☆ Then there are the death roads of Britain and Continental Europe. Visiting or retracing some of these features can be just as romantic and intriguing an outdoor pursuit as the old Watkinsian notion of ley hunting. It also offers the added satisfaction of helping to keep a particular type of relic of our heritage from disappearing out of sight and out of mind. The work falls into two parts – first, visiting known locations.

In Holland, you can visit and walk extant, strikingly straight *doodwegen* on Westerheide, near Hilversum. In Germany, an exciting cable-car ride will take you to the summit of the Wurmberg in the Harz Mountains, where you will be able to see and follow the somewhat eerie *Steinweg*. In Britain, there are a host of corpse ways to trace. One of my favourites is the so-called St Levan's Path in Cornwall. If you visit the ancient St Levan's church near Land's End, within its even older churchyard, you will see a large, dramatically cleft boulder. This was doubtless an important pagan feature, but was Christianised a millennium ago by the erection of an old Celtic cross alongside it. This is really the ancient heart of this site. Then go to the north-east entrance of the church-yard. There you will find a small Celtic cross on the wall, and in the middle of the entrance a full-sized, coffin-shaped stone. This should alert you to the fact that you are at the end of a death road. Walk along the path beyond, over a stile, and you will see a straight path cutting across the field in front of you. This is St Levan's Path. Half a mile along it you will encounter another small Celtic cross. This was part of a network of 'coffin lines' that crossed the medieval landscape of Land's End.

Another charming corpse way can be found at map grid reference SP 314396 near the village of Lower Brailes on the northern edge of the Cotswolds, four miles east of Shipston-on-Stour. Here, a corpse way runs towards the great church in the village, and descends to cross a stream. This is known locally as the 'Ninety-Nine Steps', and it still has the remains of old paving on it. Local oral tradition states that the path is a death road that runs for over 20 miles westwards to the prehistoric earthworked Bredon Hill in Gloucestershire.

☆ The second aspect of tracing death roads and corpse ways is to find and map forgotten ones. To do this, you will have to select a village in a relatively unspoiled country loca-tion, and study all you can about local folk traditions to do with death, burial, funerals, and related topics in the local reference library. When you find a reference that might indicate a corpse way, get a large-scale map, and see if you can trace where it runs. Then do your fieldwork. Another useful research procedure at the reference library or County Records Office is to check field-name maps, looking for 'Churchway Field' or similar names.

9

Mythic
Geography

The ancient lay of the land, what some enthusiasts used to call 'geomancy', is an important aspect of earth mysteries. What is in the natural landscape can be as informative as a sacred monument, because to people of the ancient world the land was their sacred text. They could refer to it, and sometimes it spoke to them.

Land and Sea as Memory Banks

Tribal myths were stored in the environment. We are perhaps best aware of this with regard to Australian Aborigine traditions. According to these, in the *tjukuba* or Dreamtime, the Earth was initially flat and uninhabited. Then giant totemic beings and creation heroes emerged. They formed the country that can now be seen by their activities: hills, ridges, trees, water holes, rocks and caves are not mere topography but also a mythic landscape. So a distinctive, domed rock outcrop is the protruding cranium of a Dreamtime being, or a cluster of boulders the Dreamtime droppings of a totemic being!

Similar mythic geographical systems are used by South Pacific islanders for their ocean navigation. In one scheme, Puluwat navigators mentally project the shape of the trigger fish on to their native seascape. The navigator imagines his base position as the centre of the fish's backbone, and uses this as a mental reference point as he sails by the positions of the stars. He notes physical features such as reefs and islands and sandbanks, as would appear on a Western naval chart, but can also include mythical items such as an imaginary frigate bird seen in rough water, a vanishing island, and a place where an imaginary whale with two tails can be seen. Systems like this encode detailed information about the ocean environment that would tend to be missed by the average Western observer, as well as about the tribal myths.

There are many other types of mythic geography, each with its own cultural twist. In their native territory of northern California, the Wintu Indians find their way through the country by means of 'guide rocks', which are distinctive boulders perched on cliffs or a rocky outcrop. Rivers are also often used to determine the cardinal orientations, and their names sometimes indicate their direction of flow. The spirit of a newly dead Wintu must travel northwards through the territory to the sacred Mount Shasta or to a spring known only to the dead. The Western Apache of Arizona use legends attached to places as a way of controlling social behaviour. So if someone in the tribe misbehaves, the elders will tell a story associated with a place in the tribal territory that holds an appropriate meaning for the transgressor. In this way, the place 'shoots an arrow' at the person, admonishing him or her and offering guidance. That place and that person always have a special relationship thereafter. The Hindu pilgrim who visits a sacred area follows a map that traces out the 'faithscape' there. So, for instance, pilgrims to

Chitrakut can obtain a special map that depicts various symbolic representations of the topography, conveying mythic information about Lord Rama's activities in this territory. The Celts also invested their home landscapes with myth. A relic of this is the pagan Celtic Irish text, the *Dindshenchas*, 'The Lore of Places'.

Elements of mythic geography have survived into recent times even in the West. The mythical island of Hy Brasil, for instance, supposedly off the west coast of Ireland, was shown on Irish naval charts until 1830. The magical island was considered to be visible from the Arran Islands in Galway Bay every seven years. One fellow claimed to have seen it in 1872, and to have made a sketch of it. He even had witnesses!

As with ancient societies, the tribal memory of traditional peoples today also tends to be externalised in the landscape, so it follows that if their territories are altered or destroyed by modern incursions, such people soon become mythic amnesiacs, and their social identity and tribal cohesion is put at risk.

Giants in the Earth

The landscape not only acted as a mythic memory bank for ancient peoples, it was also a picture gallery in which the images of gods, goddesses and cultural heroes could be discerned. This was achieved by means of *simulacra*. A simulacrum is a coincidental likeness such as a cloud in the sky appearing like a castle, the bark of a tree conjuring the appearance of a human face, or the glowing embers of a fire appearing like a golden city with spires. It is a dream-like manner of seeing that seems to have been common in many ancient cultures.

Remarkable examples of this form of mythic vision have recently been discovered by academic Egyptologist Anthony Donohue. In 1991, while he was studying the New Kingdom temple of Queen Hatshepsut at Deir el-Bahri near the Valley of the Kings, he suddenly realised that a column of rock protruding from the cliff behind the temple contained the greatly eroded image of a cobra, an important dynastic symbol in ancient Egypt, rearing over a human form wearing the head-dress and ceremonial beard of a pharaoh. Despite being so heavily eroded, this colossal figure group, hundreds of feet high, is still discernible for those who have the eyes to see it, yet it had stood unnoticed for thousands of years. Further technical investigation will be required to ascertain if it is an untouched simulacrum or a group of suggestive natural configurations that were enhanced by human hand. Whichever is the case, the ancient Egyptians had to have originally perceived the likenesses in the cliff, which suggests that they must have looked at their natural environment for symbolic meaning. Either they projected into the natural forms an expression of their own religious ideas, or, more startlingly, the surroundings may have actually suggested the royal and religious iconography we associate with dynastic Egypt. Donohue has gone on to identify several other temple locations along the Nile that are similarly marked by rock-face simulacra, showing that the Deir el-Behri case is not a one-off accident.

A similar type of rock image occurs at the Externsteine rocks in Germany. These are weathered fingers of sandstone, 100 or more feet in height, near Detmold. They have been frequented since pagan times, and contain a range of mysterious features such as a rock-hewn chapel near the top of the tallest pillar which also has a large bas-relief carved into its base showing Christ's descent from the cross, presumably representing a medieval Christianisation of the site. On one of the rock columns there is an overhanging segment that looks strikingly like a man with his arms raised, as if tied to the rock. This phenomenon has long been noted and there have been suggestions that it represents Odin hanging on the World Tree seeking the wisdom of the runes. This pagan Norse image of course carries echoes of Christ on the cross, and there is an artificial hole in the side of the Externsteine rock figure that seemingly represents the spear wound inflicted on Christ during the crucifixion. It could be, therefore, that at the time the bas-relief was being carved, someone made this hole to convert the natural rock figure from a pagan to a Christian image.

Some landscape figures could be very large in scale, involving hills and mountains, or even whole ranges. In the Americas, several ancient Dreamtime visions within the topography are known of. One example can be found in the Chisos Mountains on the Texas–Mexico border, where a mountain displays the likeness of an Indian profile, and represents a mythic figure to the Apache. In Java, Indonesia,

Profile of an Apache Dreamtime hero, in the Chisos Mountains, Texas.

the great temple of Borobodur is so positioned that part of the Menoreh mountain range visible to the south looks like a man on his back. Local folklore has it that this is Gunadharma, the original architect of the temple. It is widely thought that this topo-mythic factor was involved in the siting decision of the original holy place that preceded the present temple structure.

Landscapes of the Goddess

The Earth Mother Goddess manifests in landscape configurations that were revered by ancient peoples in Europe. In the eastern Mediterranean region mountains had long been associated with the Great Goddess — holy peaks often had ritual caves near them for goddess rituals. This reverence continued into Bronze and Iron Age Crete and Greece. From the palace temple of Knossos, Crete, for instance, the peak of Mount Juktas dominates the skyline to the south. It is a cleft or split peak, reminiscent of a pair of horns, and it can be no coincidence that great stone sculptures of horns were found there, along with murals depicting the dangerous ritual of bull-leaping. The pair of horns was just part of a whole symbolic complex, though, for the shape also suggested the raised arms gesture common in goddess ceremony throughout the eastern Mediterranean countries, a pair of breasts, and also the lap of the goddess. Eleusis, the Temple of the Mysteries west of Athens, is overlooked by Mount Kerata which has a distinctive cleft peak, while the twin-summit Mount Hymettos is visible from the Acropolis in Athens. There are numerous other examples.

The perception of a female form in the landscape reaches back to the Stone Age. From Callanish, an important group of stone circles on the Scottish Isle of Lewis, the eastern skyline is occupied by the Pairc Hills and resembles the form of a reclining woman. Sometimes called the 'Sleeping Beauty', her Gaelic name is *Cailleach na Mointeach*, the Old Woman of the Moors, a pseudonym for the Hag or Earth Mother. She is well known to the present inhabitants of the Callanish area and was doubtless so to the people who built the stone circles. Every 18.61 years, the time in the lunar cycle known as the Major Standstill, the moon rises out of the hills as if the Earth Mother is giving birth to it, and skims the horizon appearing to set amongst the stones. Further south is the Scottish island of Jura, which has a range of mountains called the Paps ('Breasts') of Jura, on account of two rounded, breast-like peaks in their midst. The summer solstice sun appears to set into the Paps when viewed from the standing stones group at Ballochroy on the Kintyre peninsula. To experience sightlines like this is to feel for a moment that one is seeing through the eyes of Stone Age people.

These kinds of landscape likeness prove that even the myths and visions of former peoples still survive. They are the monuments of ancient dreams, dreams that can be recalled to our minds if we learn how to look in the appropriate manner.

Train Your Mythic Eye

The more you try to look in this mythic way at the natural landscape surrounding ancient sacred sites during your monumenteering sessions, the more likely it is that you will learn to see like ancient people did, and to be surprised by unexpected and fascinating features that are not evident at first glance. Look closely, for a sacred site is often placed so that a hilltop or rock outcrop that had significance for the ancient users of the place is barely visible, perhaps just showing above an intervening ridge, or in a mountain notch. When you spy such a feature, try to understand what its meaning might have been.

This type of perception is aided by adopting a Dreamtime state of mind; in fact, the nature of information received through the senses is always dependent on state of mind.

EXERCISE: DREAMTIME

There are a number of ways in which Dreamtime perception can be trained. One of the most effective is to venture into a park or wild place just before sunset.

☆ Select a craggy rock, or a gnarled old tree or dead tree trunk, or even a dense bush.

☆ Settle yourself comfortably, calm your mind, breathe deeply and evenly.

☆ As twilight gathers and turns into gloaming, focus steadily on your chosen object. In the fading light the object of your attention will offer different aspects of itself. It may fleetingly look like a face, a figure, a crouching animal, a dark monster.

☆ When a form-shift like this happens, try to 'freeze' it and see the object only in that mythic way for as long as you can. When the mundane physical form re-establishes itself in your mind, allow the shape-shifting sequence to start again, and repeat the exercise. Seeing is not accomplished only with the eye.

10

Other Earth
Mysteries Themes

It has been possible to look at only some of the more important aspects of Earth Mysteries in this brief guide, so in this final chapter we will touch on a selection of a few further themes and exercises. In each case I offer an evaluation based on my years of involvement and study, for there is little point in carrying false ideas into the new millennium if what we really want to do is distil for our times the nearly lost knowledge and wisdom that has bubbled up in the past millennia. It is time for a new, better-founded generation of Earth Mysteries research.

Ancient Astronaut Theories

While there is a lack of any objective evidence for the presence of extraterrestrial beings in the remote past, there is no shortage of *interpretations* of archaeological and anthropological material by those who want to find ancient astronauts lurking in prehistory. Evidence and interpretation are two different matters. The evidence proffered by ancient astronaut proponents only seems to work because they make very narrow selections of material from the archaeological record. This does not necessarily make such people dishonest – they may be genuine in their beliefs, but they are inadequately informed. We have already noted, for instance, that ideas about ancient astronauts having made the Nazca lines can be shown to be false for a number of reasons, notably that the surface of the Nazca pampa is so sensitive that there would have to be other markings visible than merely the lines, and, more importantly, we now know that the Nazca lines are merely one example of many 'line' features throughout the Americas, some in terrain that simply cannot support the thesis of landing strips for ancient spacecraft.

The best evidence for ancient extraterrestrial contact I have seen has been provided by Robert Temple (see Further Reading). He highlights the Dogon people of the West African country of Mali who believe that their culture derived from the Nommo, amphibious creatures from Sirius who landed in 'arks' in the Middle East long ago. Temple makes a scholarly attempt to assemble evidence to support this belief as being a real memory of an encounter with extra-terrestrials. Even so, critics have given numerous reasons why Temple's ideas are mistaken.

There are without doubt anomalies and wonders in the archaeological and anthropological records – hence the exist-ence of Earth Mysteries interest – but that does not mean we have to seek answers in terms of extraterrestrial contact. The wrong answer is worse than no answer. Anyone standing before the Great Pyramid or the remarkable prehistoric stone cities of South America has to marvel at the masonry and engineering skills involved in such structures, but we should not dismiss the natural genius of human beings. As discussed, skills come and go as they are needed in the history of cultures. The genuine understanding of the spiritual and ritual life of human beings through the ages is eclipsed by modern, high-tech, mechanistic notions. It is the same kind of mentality that we have already noted emerged in North America when the European settlers speculated about the Indian mounds and earthworks as being the product of the lost tribes of Israel or wandering Atlanteans. The Indians were savages, the reasoning went, so how could their ancestors have made these great structures? Ancient astronaut theory can be seen as a sci-fi form of racism.

Atlantis and Lost Civilisations

Much the same can be said about notions regarding the 'fingerprints' of Atlanteans and other denizens of lost high civilisations that supposedly existed before the dawn of history. It was noted in Chapter 1 that Atlantis was a tale that appeared in the writings of Plato, and which he used as an illustration of his philosophical ideas. Over the centuries there have been countless suggestions of where Atlantis was situated, the prime one being, naturally, in the Atlantic ocean. We now know this cannot be true, because the floor of that ocean is well mapped and there is no evidence of a submerged continent; nor does the geological and tectonic situation allow for there having been one. The detailed 'history' of Atlantis, including its destruction by natural forces unleashed by the malevolent high-technology of its inhabitants, comes solely from modern occult sources – the visions of Edgar Cayce, for example, or claims by leaders of the occult society known as the Theosophists at the turn of the 20th century. There is no physical evidence of a lost Atlantic continent. The reason why the notion of supposed lost continents like Atlantis, Mu (Pacific Ocean), or Lemuria

(Indian Ocean) was taken seriously for a time by some scientists and scholars was because an explanation was needed to account for the spread of certain animal species and to account for particular geological similarities in some regions of the world. But this was before knowledge of plate tectonics, in which sections of the Earth's crust move over long periods of time thus creating continental drift. This new knowledge has made theories of lost continents redundant in a scientific sense, even if the need continues among occultists and romantic fantasists.

While it is just within the bounds of possibility that an advanced civilisation *did* rise and fall long before the last Ice Age, there is no true evidence of this, and it did not need to have existed to explain what we know about civilisation today. In his book, *The Lost Civilisations of the Stone Age* (1998), Richard Rudgley has collected a great deal of evidence to show that astronomical, medical and other knowledge that we consider to be advanced was clearly present and developing in the Old Stone Age or Palaeolithic era. This approach reclaims our genuine human heritage from the grip of ancient Altantean or extraterrestrial gods. It is our own, human fingerprints that are all over our past.

It is likely, however, that there were terrible natural cataclysms down the ages that left a traumatic mark on humanity's collective memory. One explanation that has been put forward to account for Atlantis, for instance, is the huge volcanic explosion that destroyed the former Mediterranean island (now a caldera) of Santorini during the Bronze Age. Another proposal is that the British Isles and the north-west coastal areas of France are what remain of a continental shelf area that was inundated by the sea about 5,000 years ago. There is surprisingly good evidence to support this, and if this is the case, then the megalithic sites scattered through Brittany, Ireland, and Britain can be seen, in a sense, to be survivals from 'Atlantis'.

The true power of the Atlantis myth is psychological in nature. It represents a yearning for a lost paradisal golden age that haunts the human psyche. That golden age is really a metaphor for a heightened state of consciousness that we usually refer to as mystical. Atlantis is submerged deep within the human unconscious.

Crop Circles

For some people the wonderful designs and patterns that have appeared in the cereal crop fields of southern England and elsewhere in the closing decades of the 20th century have become the epitome of Earth Mysteries. Here was real physical evidence of the marvellous and unexplained. Theories abounded: were they markings left by extraterrestrial craft landing overnight? Shades of ancient astronauts and Atlantis hovered near, for many of the crop circles appeared in areas with high concentrations of megalithic sites, such as Stonehenge and Avebury. Was Planet Earth, Gaia, leaving her human offspring messages in the crop fields? Or were they markings formed by a rare and as yet unstudied geophysical phenomenon taking the form of mysterious vortices in the air causing electro-magnetic side-effects?

Much excitement prevailed, with people rushing into the countryside to see the latest visions to have appeared. Specialist magazines were created to service the public interest generated, and best-selling books, tours and TV films proliferated. Crop circles shunted aside the Loch Ness Monster as the mystery to provide 'silly season' padding on news bulletins during the summer. However, it seems all happy and innocent things must come to a close, and the crop circle mystery has indeed been solved for all but the die-hard enthusiasts who evince a deep psychological need to believe in them.

In 1991, two elderly artists, Doug Bower and Dave Chorley, announced that they had produced the original crop circle formations and a number of the later ones. They said that they had been inspired by 'flying saucer nests', rough circular depressions in grass, claimed by UFOlogists years before to be where UFOs had landed. Doug and Dave had done it for fun, and to see if they could cause a public stir. The mainstream press screamed their story, and general interest in crop circles started to wane. Crop circle enthusiasts were not pleased, however, and remained unconvinced. Surely no human being could create these wonderful, intricate patterns, let alone at the dead of night? Well, tests in 1992 proved that they could. Gradually additional hoaxers came forth, Doug and Dave produced further in-depth evidence of their work, and it became clear that the intelligence that had been at work in the summer fields was human. Attempts to find holes in the hoax explanation have been legion, and some of them have had the trappings of science, but all have been shown to be wanting, or flawed, or have been directly refuted.

Crop formations still appear, showing ever more sophistication, and the believers still visit them to wonder and speculate and to escape the mundanity of everyday life. But this has its costs. In 1996, pseudo-symbols taken from crop marking imagery were sprayed with black paint on to some of the venerable old stones of Avebury. This New Age vandalism was in its way an instructive metaphor: all too often false mysteries obscure the real ones, directing attention, time and energy away on to dead-end trails.

Dowsing

Dowsing is the ability to detect underground water, metals, and other things by means of a little-understood body-mind sensing ability. The method traditionally involved the use of a springy forked twig, but tensioned dowsing rods or the pendulum have become popular. These tools amplify the dowser's small muscular movements when he or she unconsciously reacts to a dowsing target. From what limited research there has been, the mechanism involved in on-site field dowsing seems to relate to a human sensitivity to quite subtle changes in local magnetic and possibly electric fields, though this has still to be confirmed. Dowsing from maps may be a completely different phenomenon that has simply been included under the general term of 'dowsing'.

Dowsing is a real human faculty, but its occurrence tends to be inconsistent even among the few who can practise it with any real level of skill, and the claims surrounding it far exceed what it is actually is capable of – dowsers are no more immune from fantasies and pet theories than any other sector of the human population.

Dowsing has become far more associated with Earth Mysteries than any reason or evidence warrants. The main connection has been its spurious use to support claims about energies in ley lines, as mentioned earlier. Experiments I have conducted have yet to show anyone capable of finding subtle natural energies in any reliable fashion, yet books abound with the most detailed dowsing claims about the supposed energy properties of ley lines and standing stones. Genuine localised magnetic and electrical anomalies can be picked up by a few rare, good dowsers, but the more fantastic claims are without foundation. Indeed, as with the crop circles, they have led to vandalism: the ground plan of the only example of a stone labyrinth site in Britain (on the Scilly Isles) was altered by a group of New Age energy dowsers who convinced themselves that the feature had originally been used to mark out earth forces and that these had now changed their configuration. How did these individuals know all this? Because their dowsing rods told them.

If you wish to develop your dowsing skills, proceed (and read) with caution, and ensure that your results are objective rather than simply what you want them to be. Start out by selecting your dowsing tool. I advise the good, old-fashioned springy twig, as pendulums and what are called angle-rods can far too easily be almost subconsciously manipulated to obtain a particular result – I've done it myself! Get someone to secretly prepare ten containers of water, in just one of which there is dissolved a pinch of salt, and spread them out over the floor, lawn or yard. Your helper must know which container has the salted water. Without the helper being present, try to dowse the container holding the salted water. Repeat this exercise until you can find the target with reasonable frequency first time. If you consistently fail, then use your time to better advantage on something else.

Sacred Geometry

Sacred or *canonical* geometry is based on patterns found in nature, ranging from the logarithms of growth in plants and organisms to the geometry inherent in the vibration of atoms and molecules and in the motion of planets and stars. Because of this, it was of significance to temple builders, who wished to encode into their structures the ratios of creation. Sacred architecture was about creating a model of the universe on a small scale – a microcosm of the macrocosm.

Sacred geometry requires only straight-edge and compass,

for it is to do with ratio and proportion, not quantitative measure by number. By this means, it is possible to design your very own Great Pyramid! This has been shown in the works of John Michell. Referring to the diagram shown below, start with a pair of compasses by drawing two circles centred on a line BA so that they overlap, with the circumference of the one passing through the centre of the other. The overlapping segment is known as the vesica piscis, the 'vessel of the fish', due to its shape. (It was a secret sign of the Christians in the catacombs.) Then put your compass point on A and pencil on B and swing an arc, XY. Repeat the procedure, using B as a centre, thus creating a larger vesica shape. Next, draw the rhombus XBYA. This cuts the circles at C and D as shown. These points and the bottom of the

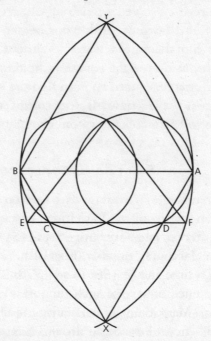

Great Pyramid Geometry (after John Michell)

smaller vesica form a horizontal line. Join them up with a ruler, and extend the line until it meets the larger arcs at E and F, as shown. Draw lines from these points to meet at the top of the smaller vesica.

The triangle produced matches the profile of the Great Pyramid. If you have performed these geometric procedures with care and accuracy, you should be able to take a protractor and find that the base angles of your triangle are close to 55 degrees, 51 minutes, the mean base angles of the Great Pyramid at Giza. Now all you have to do is cut a few million cubic metres of stone accurately into shape and build your own . . .

Terrestrial Zodiacs

This is one of those quirky ideas that can be found in the undergrowth of Earth Mysteries themes. The idea of giant zodiacal designs laid out over miles of countryside is older than modern Earth Mysteries, in fact. After studying airviews and maps of the Glastonbury area in the 1920s, artist Katherine Maltwood came to the conclusion that certain topographical features formed a ten-mile-wide circle of zodiacal effigies centred near the village of Butleigh. She became convinced that this was the reality of the Round Table in the legends of King Arthur and published her ideas in *Glastonbury's Temple of the Stars* (1935) and other works. The concept of terrestrial zodiacs was championed and developed by later researchers, notably Elizabeth Leader and Mary Caine. For a time in the 1960s and 1970s, numerous claims for the existence of several such supposed features were put forward, and Mary Caine in particular has argued extensively for the existence of a zodiac around Kingston-on-Thames. Sceptics point out that the figures comprising them are marked out by river courses, ancient roads, dykes, bound-aries of woodland, and other features which have appeared at different times in the landscape, thus negating the possibility that they could delineate a single concept, and in any case some of these landscape features have changed over the years – woodland changes its shape, for example, and rivers silt up in some places and carve new courses over time causing radical changes in their meandering.

A scattering of place names and place-related legends have been found at appropriate spots on the Glastonbury and Kingston zodiacs, among others, and this has been presented as confirmatory evidence by terrestrial zodiac protagonists. But if various images can be seen in an inkblot, think how a map provides a much richer matrix out of which patterns can be drawn. It proves easier than might be thought to glimpse 'zodiacs' on a number of one-inch or 1:50,000-scale maps of Britain. I recall once perceiving a terrestrial zodiac on a map of the Leicestershire–Derbyshire border, and was elated when my field investigations came up with a pub called The Ram in the bit of countryside I had identified as the Aries figure.

It is fun to do a little 'zodiac-spotting' on maps, and even in the field, but while some psychological and poetic validity can be granted to perceived terrestrial zodiacs, this should not be confused with them being actual physical features fashioned with human intent on the landscape in ages past. Terrestrial zodiacs simply reflect our own, modern, map-trained minds.

World Centre

Despite seeming odd to modern Western sensibilities, this concept is an exceedingly ancient one, deeply rooted in the human psyche, and is a core element of ancient wisdom. Essentially, the theme refers to the ancient concept of a symbolic World Centre, known in the literature as the *omphalos*, World Navel, and World Axis, among other terms. It was an image that ordered time and space for earlier peoples and could operate at many scales – landscape, town, temple, society, body, and mind – and was integral to religious cosmologies and myth.

The concept has appeared in most ancient and traditional cultures in all periods of human history, and has taken numerous forms. A famous example is the *mundus* of the ancient Etruscans of northern Italy, which was a pit dug at the centre of their cities from which the usually grid-iron street plan was laid out. This pit was mythically linked to the underworld, and was capped by a large stone which was lifted on special days when the dead were allowed to mingle with the living. The Romans absorbed this basic idea and carried it around the world in the laying out of their settlements. The ancient Greeks placed special domed stones at their temples known as *omphaloi*, navel stones. Jerusalem holds a special status as World Navel to Judiasm, Islam and Christianity alike; medieval Christian maps placed Jerusalem in their centres. In northern Europe and Asia, the World Centre was usually envisaged as either the pole star, or as a World Tree. The Siberian shaman was believed to go to the World Tree while in trance and climb or descend its trunk in order to move 'between the worlds'. The best-known example of a World Tree is probably the Norse *Yggdrasil*, the World Ash, on which Odin hung to gain the knowledge of the runes. The maypole contains an echo of the World Tree idea.

In some cultures the World Centre is represented as a hill or mountain. The pagan Celts of Ireland, for instance, chose the hill of Usineach, County Westmeath, as their World Centre, the point where the four ancient provinces of Ulster, Munster, Leinster and Connacht met. A large natural boulder called *Aill na Mireann*, the 'Stone of Divisions' is to be found on the hill's slopes. Hindu cosmology has the mythic Mount Meru (physically embodied in the Himalayan peak of Mount Kailas) standing at the centre of the world. In Cambodia, the walls and moats of the city of Angkor Wat represent the world surrounded by its chain of mountains and the cosmic ocean, and the temple in the centre represents Mount Meru. In India and south-east Asia, whole towns were built in the image of the universe, with a symbolic representation of Mount Meru in their centres taking the form of a temple.

The idea of the World Centre also occurs in the Americas. The concept of 'Centre Place' is very important in Pueblo Indian cosmology – as an example, the Tewa of New Mexico consider their oldest pueblo village as occupying 'Earth Mother, Earth Navel, Middle Place'. A small hole in the floor of all Pueblo Indian kivas (ceremonial chambers) is called the *sipapu*, and symbolises the point from which the original Pueblo peoples emerged from the ground.

Mount Harney in South Dakota has been identified as the mountain peak to which the Oglala Sioux holy man, Black Elk, was transported during his Great Vision. This was full of powerful symbolism of the World Centre, and the Six Directions – north, south, east, west, up ('sky') and down ('earth'). Although Harney Peak was the physical representation of the World Axis for his experience, wise old Black Elk remarked that 'anywhere is the centre of the world'. This is because the concept is essentially a projection of human physiology. The human being is an axis at the meeting point of the four bodily directions of front, back, left and right.

Projected, these become the prime Four Directions of north, south, west and east. The great psychologist C.G. Jung referred to this 'centring process and a radial arrangement' as being archetypal within the human psyche. It enabled ancient people to order their physical environment and divide the skyline. This made possible the measurement of time by observing the movement of the sun, moon and other heavenly bodies along the horizon.

The World Centre concept is therefore essentially an ancient and mythic way of talking about *here*. 'Here' is portable, it can exist anywhere and everywhere, hence Black Elk's comment. 'Here' is always the centre – it is where you always are, it is where we all always are. Stand on a beach, a desert or moorland and look how the horizon encircles you. Build a circle of stones to reflect that, and stand within it. Inwardly, the World Centre where the Four Directions meet is the crack between the worlds, the place where communication with spirits and gods is possible. Outwardly, it is the reference point for ordering the earth and the heavens, space and time.

In our frenetic modern world, with its linear time and abstract knowledge about the world, we have lost the experience of that stabilising centre. We are lost in space. Perhaps the most important element of ancient wisdom we can try to recapture at both personal and cultural levels is that healing point known as the World Centre. Our culture desperately needs to centre itself.

Useful Addresses

Paul Devereux

For further information on books, events, courses and news of Earth Mysteries, or to contact the author with general queries, write to: Paul Devereux, PO Box 11, Moreton-in-Marsh, Gloucestershire, GL56 0ZF or access his website at http://www.acemake.com/PaulDevereux

Websites

www.leyhunter.com
The site covers geomancy, Earth Mysteries, ancient wisdom and sacred sites.

www.thirdstone.demon.co.uk
This looks at all aspects of antiquarianism including ancient sites, archaeology and paganism, with links to other related sites.

Journals

3rd *Stone*, The Magazine for the New Antiquarian, Box 961, Devizes, Wiltshire SN10 2TS.
E-mail: njm@thirdstone.demon.co.uk

Caerdroia, The Journal of Mazes and Labyrinths, 53 Thundersley Grove, Thundersley, Essex SS7 3EB.
E-mail: Caerdroia@dial.pipex.com

Magonia, Interpreting Contemporary Vision and Belief, 5 James Terrace, London SW14 8HB

RILKO Journal, Journal of the Research into Lost Knowledge Organisation, 43 Dorchester Avenue, London N13 5DY

Site Saver, Newsletter of the Sacred Sites International Foundation, 1442A Walnut Street, #330 Berkeley, CA 94709–1405.
E-mail: sacredsite@aol.com

Source, The Holy Wells Journal, Swn-y-Mor, 96 Terrace Road, Mount Pleasant, Swansea SA1 6HU.

Further Reading

There are thousands of books currently available on Earth Mysteries topics. As it is possible to show only a tiny sample here, I have included those that I think would be the most helpful. While your bookseller will be able to supply some, you may have to order others through your local library. Most of the titles listed contain extensive bibliographies to enable you to research further as you wish – I have included some of my own books in certain categories for this specific reason.

Ancient Astronomy

Brennan, Martin, *The Stars and the Stones*, Thames and Hudson, 1983

Krupp, E.C., *Skywatchers, Shamans and Kings*, John Wiley, 1997

Thom, A., *Megalithic Sites in Britain*, Oxford University Press, 1967

Williamson, Ray, A., and Farrer, Claire R., *Earth and Sky*, University of New Mexico Press, 1992

Ancient Sacred Sites

Burl, Aubrey, *The Stone Circles of the British Isles*, Yale University Press, 1976

Burl, Aubrey, *From Carnac to Callanish*, Yale University Press, 1993

Chippindale, Christopher, *Stonehenge Complete* (first edn, 1983), Thames and Hudson, 1994

Devereux, Paul, *Secrets of Ancient and Sacred Places*, Blandford Press, 1992

Frazier, Kendrick, *People of Chaco*, W.W. Norton, 1986

Mohen, Jean-Pierre, *The World of Megaliths*, Cassell, 1989

Palmer, Martin, and Palmer, Nigel, *Sacred Britain*, Piatkus, 1997

Thomas, David Hurst, *Exploring Ancient Native America*, Macmillan, 1994

Atlantis and Lost Civilisations

Dunbavin, Paul, *The Atlantis Researches* (first edn, 1992), Third Millennium, 1995

Rudgley, Richard, *Lost Civilisations of the Stone Age*, Century, 1998

Dowsing

Bailey, Richard N., Cambridge, Eric, and Briggs, H. Denis, *Dowsing and Church Archaeology*, Intercept, 1988

Bird, Christopher, *Divining*, Raven/Macdonald and Jane's, 1979

Whitlock, Ralph, *Water Divining*, David & Charles, 1982

Earth Energies

Devereux, Paul, *Places of Power* (first edn, 1990), Blandford Press, 1999

General Earth Mysteries

Dames, Michael, *Mythic Ireland*, Thames and Hudson, 1992

Devereux, Paul, *The Illustrated Encyclopedia of Ancient Earth Mysteries*, Blandford Press, 2000

Eitel, E.J., *Feng Shui* (first edn, 1873), Cokaygne, 1973 (There have been more recent editions.)

Gimbutas, Marija, *The Language of the Goddess*, Thames and Hudson, 1989

Grinsell, Leslie V., *Folklore of Prehistoric Sites in Britain*, David & Charles, 1976

Hodges, Peter (Julian Keable, ed.), *How the Pyramids Were Built*, Element Books, 1989

Lip, Evelyn, *Chinese Geomancy* (first edn, 1979), Times Books International, 1994

MacManus, Dermot, *The Middle Kingdom* (first edn, 1959), Colin Smyth, 1973

Michell, John, *The Earth Spirit*, Thames and Hudson, 1975

Temple, Robert K., *The Sirius Mystery*, BCA, 1976 (There is a considerably more recent edition.)

Weatherhill, Craig, and Devereux, Paul, *Myths and Legends of Cornwall*, Sigma, 1994

Ley Hunting

Devereux, Paul, *The New Ley Hunter's Guide*, Gothic Image, 1994 (and the *Encyclopedia*, as above)

Michell, John, *The Old Stones of Land's End*, Garnstone Press, 1974

Pennick, Nigel, and Devereux, Paul, *Lines on the Landscape*, Robert Hale, 1989

Watkins, Alfred, *The Old Straight Track*, Methuen, 1925 (There have been numerous more recent editions.)

Watkins, Alfred, *The Ley Hunter's Manual* (first edn, 1927), Turnstone Press, 1983

Sacred Geometry and Arcane Knowledge

Critchlow, Keith, *Time Stands Still*, Gordon Fraser, 1979
Huntley, H.E., *The Divine Proportion*, Dover, 1970
Lawlor, Robert, *Sacred Geometry*, Thames and Hudson, 1982
Michell, John, *The Dimensions of Paradise*, Thames and Hudson, 1988
Sterling, William, *The Canon* (first edn, 1897), Garnstone Press, 1974

Shamanism, Shamanic Landscapes and Related Subjects

Aveni, Anthony (ed.), *The Lines of Nazca*, The American Philosophical Society, 1990
Davidson, Hilda Ellis (ed.), *The Seer*, John Donald, 1989
Devereux, Paul, *Shamanism and the Mystery Lines*, Quantum, 1992; Llewellyn, 1993
Devereux, Paul, *The Long Trip*, Penguin Arkana, 1997
Dobkin de Rios, Marlene, *Hallucinogens − Cross-Cultural Perspectives* (first edn, 1984), Prism Press, 1990
Duerr, Hans Peter, *Dreamtime − Concerning the Boundary Between Wilderness and Civilization* (first edn, 1978), Blackwell, 1985
Eliade, Mircea, *Shamanism − Archaic Techniques of Ecstasy* (first edn, 1951), Bollingen, Princeton University Press, 1964
Ereira, Alan, *The Heart of the World*, Jonathan Cape, 1990
Harner, Michael J. (ed.), *Hallucinogens and Shamanism*, Oxford University Press, 1973
Hutton, Ronald, *The Pagan Religions of the Ancient British Isles*, Blackwell, 1991
Lewis-Williams, J.D., and Dowson, T.A., *Images of Power*, Southern Book Publishers, 1989
Morrison, Tony, *Pathways to the Gods*, Michael Russell, 1978
Scully, Vincent, *The Earth, The Temple, and The Gods*, Yale University Press, 1962

Psychic Archaeology

Bligh Bond, Frederick, *The Gate of Remembrance* (first edn, 1918), Thorsons, 1978
Goodman, Jeffrey, *Psychic Archaeology* (first edn, 1977), Wildwood House, 1978

Index

Piatkus Guides, written by experts, combine background information with practical exercises, and are designed to change the way you live. Titles include:

Tarot   Cassandra Eason

Tarot's carefully graded advice enables readers to obtain excellent readings from Day One. You will quickly gain a thorough knowledge of both Major and Minor Arcanas and their symbolism, and learn how to use a variety of Tarot spreads.

Meditation   Bill Anderton

Meditation covers the origins, theory and benefits of meditation. It includes over 30 meditations and provides all the advice you need to mediate successfully.

Crystal Wisdom   Andy Baggott and Sally Morningstar

Crystal Wisdom is a fascinating guide to the healing power of crystals. It details the history and most popular modern uses of crystals and vibrational healing. It also covers colour, sound and chakra healing, and gem, crystal and flower essences.

Celtic Wisdom   Andy Baggott

Celtic Wisdom is a dynamic introduction to this popular subject. The author covers Celtic spirituality, the wisdom of trees, animals and stones, ritual and ceremony and much more.

Feng Shui   Jon Sandifer

Feng Shui introduces the origins, theory and practice of the Chinese art of perfect placement, or geomancy. It provides easy-to-follow techniques to help you carry out your own readings and create an auspicious living space.

The Essential Nostradamus   Peter Lemesurier

The Essential Nostradamus charts the life of this extraordinary man, and includes newly discovered facts about his life and work. Peter Lemesurier unravels his prophecies for the coming decades.